CATALOGUE OF THE FRANCIS TRIGGE CHAINED LIBRARY
ST WULFRAM'S CHURCH, GRANTHAM

I. A corner of the Francis Trigge Chained Library in St Wulfram's Church, Grantham (Photograph by David George)

CATALOGUE OF THE FRANCIS TRIGGE CHAINED LIBRARY

ST WULFRAM'S CHURCH
GRANTHAM

JOHN GLENN
with
DAVID WALSH

John Glenn

D.S.BREWER

First published 1988 by D. S. Brewer
240 Hills Road, Cambridge
an imprint of Boydell & Brewer Ltd
PO Box 9, Woodbridge, Suffolk IP12 3DF
and of Boydell & Brewer Inc.
Wolfeboro, New Hampshire 03894-2069, USA

ISBN 0 85991 258 2

British Library Cataloguing in Publication Data

Glenn, John
Catalogue of the Francis Trigge Chained Library, St. Wulfram's Church, Grantham.
1. Francis Trigge Chained Library – Catalogue.
I. Title II. Walsh, David III. Francis Trigge Chained Library.
018'.1 Z921.G6/
ISBN 0-85991-258-2

Library of Congress Cataloging-in-Publication Data

Glenn, John.
Catalogue of the Francis Trigge Chained Library, St. Wulfram's Church, Grantham / John Glenn with David Walsh.
p. cm.
Includes index.
ISBN 0-85991-258-2
1. Francis Trigge Chained Library (Grantham, Lincolnshire) – Catalogs. 2. Trigge, Francis, 1547?–1606 – Library – Catalogs. 3. Church libraries – England – Grantham (Lincolnshire) – Catalogs. 4. Chained books – Bibliography – Catalogs. 5. Bibliography – Early printed books – Catalogs. 6. Theology – Bibliography – Catalogs. I. Walsh, David. II. Francis Trigge Chained Library (Grantham, Lincolnshire) III. Title.
Z921.G63G57 1988
027.6'7'094253–dc19 87-32634
CIP

Printed in Great Britain by Short Run Press, Exeter
Bound by Short Run Press, Exeter

CONTENTS

Dedicated to the memory of Canon Horace Nelson and
Walter Mouncey, whose work of restoration
during 1893–4 saved the books of the
Trigge Library from disintegration.

Preface

This catalogue was begun, with the permission of the Rector and Churchwardens of St Wulfram's, Grantham, to record completely the contents of an ancient library of local interest that had never been fully examined. It soon became clear, as items of some rarity came to light, that the usefulness of the lists could be extended by giving more details, and the amateur compilers have now tried to give enough information in each entry to allow anyone who happens to be examining a book to decide whether or not it corresponds to a volume in our collection.

We thought it would be interesting to give the collations of works listed in those standard catalogues that do not have this information, and to record any differences noted in our copies from catalogues such as Adams which do. In the end, since we had to take off the collations before searching the catalogues, we have included them for all books, whether recorded elsewhere or not.

We hope that anyone, working on specialist bibliographies of any one writer or printer, can decide from our entries whether books are worth further investigation, without wasted enquiries or journeys in vain. We now have, moreover, what the church has so far lacked, a detailed inventory of Francis Trigge's generous benefaction and of any books that were added. We are grateful for all who have helped in the project, and have had assistance from many who have been interested in individual books, but particularly from those who put our feet on the proper paths when we began the task. We would like to thank Peter Hoare, the Librarian of Nottingham University, Joan Williams of the Cathedral Library of Lincoln and Dennis Rhodes of the British Library. Without their constant help and the facilities they made available we should still be walking in the dark.

The Friends of St Wulfram's have sponsored the publication of the catalogue, and the Council of Management of the Marc Fitch Fund have generously guaranteed us against financial loss. We were fortunate in getting the help of Barry Payne of the Grantham Information Technology Centre, who made his staff and equipment freely available to us. Janet Bayliss of the Centre and a team of Youth Training Scheme volunteers transferred our much amended typescript to the word processor and on through the latest 'desk top publishing' technology to produce camera ready copy for the catalogue entries. Without the Centre, we should still be struggling to make the text presentable.

We are also grateful to the Grantham Community Project Agency, who appointed David Walsh to St Wulfram's Church for one year as a part-time assistant. His work in dressing the covers of the books, in checking titles, collations and dates, and in preparing a card index of locations has been admirably professional.

The catalogue is now issued as a result of co-operative effort directed towards a local heritage of national importance.

J.G.

The Francis Trigge Library

In 1598 Francis Trigge, Rector of Welbourne in Lincolnshire, by a quadripartite agreement made between him, the Alderman and burgesses of Grantham, the two prebendaries of Salisbury who held the living of St Wulfram's in absence, and their two vicars, arranged for a library to be provided in the parvise of the South Porch of the church, for the use of the clergy and inhabitants of the town and the Soke.

The Alderman was to be responsible for furnishing the porchroom and Trigge undertook to supply books to the value of 'one hundereth poundes or thereaboutes'. The vicars and schoolmaster were to oversee the use of the library, and before being given keys by the Alderman took an oath to abide by the rules as set out in an attached schedule. Permission to house the library in the church was issued by the Bishop of Lincoln in 1599. All three documents are now in the Grantham Parish deposit of the Lincolnshire Archives, with one oath signed by the vicars in 1611. No earlier or later oaths are now extant.

The library was thus the first English library to be endowed outside an institution, and although housed in a church was a civic library under the control of the Borough of Grantham. Because of the very limited access allowed by the schedule of rules it is misleading to call it 'the first public library', and there is no evidence that it was ever used for systematic study.

Francis Trigge died in 1606 leaving thirteen named books to the library in his will. These are noted in the catalogue if now extant. Finally, in 1608, a '*catalogus librorum*' was prepared, listing authors and brief titles. This list is transcribed as an appendix, with the present catalogue numbers added to volumes still extant.

Although there is no direct evidence it seems that Trigge assembled the books by sending to Cambridge to buy what happened to be going. Such bindings and provenances as we can trace lead to Cambridge, which is, indeed, the nearest centre where two hundred or so books of divinity 'and other learninge' could have been obtained. About a quarter of the works are secondhand, mainly of dates prior to 1550. Many of these carry signatures, inscriptions and often marginalia in early sixteenth century hands. There are two volumes signed by Trigge, evidently given by him at the time from his own books. Some of the books seem to have been picked up cheaply without discrimination. Fourteenth century legal decisions in Italian cities such as Padua or Siena, collected in manuscript and printed on the early presses of Venice or Naples before 1500, cannot have been of much use or interest, lay or clerical, in the Soke of Grantham in the early sixteen hundreds. They are now, of course, among our rarest items.

The theological mix is also indiscriminate, and the Lutheran propaganda of the Magdeburg Centuriators shares shelf space with the refutations of Protestant theology by Cardinal Bellarmine.

There was no apparent attempt to create a small library as comprehensive as possible for the clergy who would be the main users. Among the 228 titles assembled by 1608 are five commentaries on the Psalms and five on Genesis, but only one (and that by St Albert the Great) on St Mark. None of the seven works published by Trigge himself between 1589 and 1602 is included. We have three very early volumes of Canon Law and Decretals with commentaries (1488, 1505, 1514). It is difficult not to assume that these came on the market after the Dissolution.

During the later seventeenth century a few books were added, notably the works of Grantham born Henry More, donated by the author. The library is mentioned briefly by Anthony Wood in *Athenae Oxonienses* (1691); then it disappears from even informal records till early in the nineteenth century when T. F. Dibdin visited it and noted its deplorable condition. There are a few other short accounts of the library, notably one by Sir Gilbert Scott who redesigned the interior of the church during 1863–1866. Scott recorded some of the earliest books – the first essay towards a systematic listing since 1608.

In 1881 Samuel Rudd dismantled the decaying floor and leaking roof of the Porch Room and rebuilt them as a memorial to his daughter who had died some years earlier. The presses now occupied by the books date from this time, and the remaining chains were attached to rods on each press.

The books were once chained to the earlier benches, but only 82 chains remain. There are also four unattached chains extant, two of them in the museum at Grantham. The rest, with all the original brass clasps, have been ripped off and lost.

The books, although now well housed, remained on the shelves with covers loose and beetle larvae at work until 1893, when Canon Hector Nelson, the former principal of Lincoln Diocesan Training College (from 1862–1892), settled in Grantham and took the library in hand. He raised money locally and had the books repaired or rebound. The work was done in Grantham by William Mouncey, employed as a binder by a small family business making account books. The repaired books were arranged more suitably on the shelves, the fading fore-edge titles were rewritten (not very elegantly) and eleven parcels were made up of coverless books not considered to be worth rebinding but which, in Canon Nelson's own words, 'should not be destroyed'. One of these parcels contained a Johannes de Milis *Repertorium* (*in jure canonico*), Basel 1488, complete save for a torn colophon which would have dated it! Nelson also mentions a 'bundle of loose leaves', but there is no trace of them now and one wonders if he destroyed them. Over two hundred volumes were repaired or rebound by Mouncey in 1893/4, work that undoubtedly saved the library from disintegration. A modern conservator might have approached the repair differently, although it is unlikely that the restoration, had it been left, would ever have been attempted. Canon Nelson died in 1896.

From the turn of the century the library began to be seen by visitors, but worms continued their attacks on the oak boards unseen, and apparently un-noticed, until 1923. In this year Mrs M. Phipps, one of a group of parishioners who undertook to clean up the church interior, was allotted the parvise for her attention. She devoted her spare time to the library from then on for the next thirty years, treating the leather with preservative oil and setting up a fumigation box to deal with the worms. She began to compile a hand-list of authors, titles, printers and dates, working from an author list without dates made by Canon Nelson, but this was never expanded or published. She, and Mr Griffin who succeeded her, also had some books rebound by the Stationery Office acting for the British Museum.

In 1957 the late N. C. Ker requested information about the library for his book *The Parochial Libraries of the Church of England (1959)*, and was sent transcriptions of the founding documents by P. C. Willard, the late Borough Librarian who had discovered them in the Town Archives. These transcriptions are now deposited in the Bodleian with a copy of the Phipps list (MS Eng Misc. C.360).

Recently a display case has been set up to protect books of particular interest to visitors and the present catalogue has been compiled. The library is open to visitors at advertised times, but anyone who wishes to examine or consult the works of any authors or printers can do so by arrangement made through the Verger, St Wulfram's Church, Grantham.

A file has been prepared containing sources for a history of the library, with documents or transcripts, copies of articles and full references to information used in writing this note. It may be consulted in the Church Vestry.

A note on the Newcome Library

In 1765 John Newcome, a native of Grantham, Master of St John's College, Cambridge and Dean of Rochester, bequeathed some of his books to the Corporation to form a Parish Library, also to be kept in the church, 'for the Clergy and Gentlemen of the Neighbourhood'. These books were housed separately in a different part of the church and transferred to the Grantham Public Library in 1929.

An earlier catalogue of 1767 was reprinted by R. Storr of Grantham in 1820, and contains 500 titles. A copy is held at the King's School, Grantham.

The Newcome Library is not associated with the Trigge Library, but there is always the possibility that a book or books originally belonging to one will now be found in the other.

Arrangement and reference

Books are listed alphabetically under authors, whose names are taken from standard catalogues rather than the title pages. Anonymous works follow the first word of the title. Works bound together are noted but are numbered and catalogued separately.

Each book is referred to one of the standard catalogues, consulted in the order given below.

STC[2] Pollard, A. W. and Redgrave, G. R.: A short-title catalogue of books printed in England, Scotland and Ireland and of English books printed abroad 1475–1640. Second edition, revised and enlarged by W. A. Jackson and F. S. Ferguson, completed by C. F. Pantzer. Vols 1–2, London: Bibliographical Society, 1976–86.

Wing Wing, Donald: Short-title catalogue of books printed in England, Scotland, Ireland, Wales and British America and of English books printed in other countries 1641–1700. 3 vols, New York: Index Society, 1957.

Wing[2] Second edition, revised and enlarged. Vols 1–2, New York: Modern Language Association, 1972–82.

Adams Adams, H. M.: Catalogue of books printed on the continent of Europe 1501–1600 in Cambridge libraries. 2 vols, Cambridge: University Press, 1967.

NA–NZ The National Union Catalog, pre-1956 imprints from American libraries. 754 vols, London: Mansell, 1969–81.

A few books may be referred to

BL British Museum General Catalogue of Printed Books. 263 vols, London: British Museum, 1959–66. (Now the British Library.)

Books printed before 1500 are referred, if possible, to

BMC Catalogue of books printed in the XV century now in the British Museum. Parts 1–10, London: British Museum, 1908–1971.

Hain Hain, L.: Repertorium bibliographicum. 4 vols, 1826–38, reprinted Milano: Görlich, 1948.

Hain* Copinger, W. A.: Supplement to Hain's Repertorium bibliographicum. 3 vols, 1895–1902, reprinted Milano: Görlich, 1950.

Catalogues used once only for books not otherwise recorded are not listed above but are given in full with the book entry.

Numbers of pages or folios, if in square brackets, have been ascertained by counting, or otherwise inferred, from sections not numerated.

Authors, titles, imprints or dates in square brackets have been obtained from reference sources other than the books. Parentheses in titles or imprints show details obtained from parts of the books other than title pages, often when these are missing or incomplete. Elsewhere parentheses follow usual conventions. Bindings have been referred to

Old. Oldham, J. B.: English blind-stamped bindings. Cambridge: University Press, 1952.
Old. (P) Oldham, J. B.: Blind panels of English binders. Cambridge: University Press, 1958.

All repairs and rebindings refer to the 1894 Nelson and Mouncey programme unless described otherwise. At this time loose covers and leather panels may have been replaced on books to which they did not originally belong. Dimensions are in millimetres.

There is a card file in the Library in catalogue order which gives shelf locations.

ALBERT, Saint (Albertus Magnus, Bishop of Ratisbon, 1193-1280)

1 Postilla super Ioannis euangeliare.
(Hagenau, in officina industrij Hẽrici Gran, 1504) Fol.
AA-BB^{8} CC, DD^{6} (DD6 blank) aa-hh$^{8.8.8.6}$ ii-rr$^{8.8.6}$ ss-xx$^{8.6}$ yy^{6} zz^{8} ff[I] II-CLXVII
Adams A550. Collation differs.
Bound in with his Super Marci euangeliare postilla, 1505 (3)

2 Prima et secunda partes postille super euangeliare Luce.
(Hagenau, industrij Hẽrici Gran, 1505) Fol.
One volume in three parts:
1. Registrum super postillam
a-b^{8} c^{6} d^{8} e^{6} f^{8} (f8 blank) ff[44]
2. Prima pars
a-m$^{8.8.8.6}$ n-x$^{8.8.6}$ y^{8} (y8 blank) ff I-CLXIII
3. Secunda pars
aA, bB^{8} cC^{6} dD-fF^{8} gG^{6} hH-mM^{8} nN^{6} oO-yY^{8} zZ^{10} (zZ10 blank) ff CLXIIII-CCCXLIII
Adams A549
Blank initial for headwords with guide letter.
Foliation error: six leaves after CLXIII are CLXXIIII, CLXXV, CLXXVII, CLXIX, CLXX, CLXXIX, then CLXXX to end.
Binding Old. 490 with 597 (Reynes), repaired. 315x217

3 Super Marci euangeliare postilla.
(Hagenau, industrij Henrici Gran, 1505) Fol.
Aa^{6} (Aa6 blank) Aa, Bb^{8} Cc^{6} Dd-Gg^{8} Hh^{6} Ii-Nn^{8} (Nn8 blank) ff[8] III-XCIX
Adams A458
First 8 line initial blank with guide letter.
Signed : Liber Francis Trigge
Binding Old. 490 with 597 (Reynes), repaired. 393x252
Also bound in : Postilla super Ioannis euangeliare, 1504 (1)

ALLIACO, Petrus de (Pierre D'Ailly, 1350-1420)

4 Imago mundi (et tractatus alii). (Includes : Iohannis Gersonis opuscula varia).
[Louvain, Johannes de Westfalia, c.1483] Fol.
a-k^{8} l^{4} χ^{6} aa-ii^{8} kk^{10} 172 leaves, not numerated.
BMC IX, 146 Hain* 836
Diagrams between l and aa in this copy. Blocks of blind type on kk10 and χ6
Notes on g7 verso dated 1596, signed Kyngeston (?)
Signed on χ6 : Thomas Scarborough
Half-calf on oak boards, modern rebinding. 298x215
[For a detailed account of the parts of this book see Buron, Edmond : Ymago Mundi de Pierre D'Aill et (les) notes marginales de Christophe Colomb. (Paris, 1930)]

ALTERCATIO

5 Altercatio synagogae et ecclesiae.
Coloniae, apud Melchiorem Nouesianum, 1587 Fol.
*^{6} α^{2} A^{4} B-V^{6} ff[8] I-CXVIII
Adams A814
Title page and f1 have woodcuts. Manuscript notes and marginalia. Title page inscribed : Sum liber Robert Cook et amicoru fata diam inuenient.
Bound in with BULLINGER : Ieremais expositus, 1575 (62)

AMBROSE, Saint (Bishop of Milan, c.334-397)

6 Omnia quotquot extant D. Ambrosii Episcopi Mediolanensis opera. [Edited by Erasmus].
Basileae, [Eusebius and Nicolaus Episcopius], 1567 Fol.
5 books bound in 2 volumes:
6.1 1. A-C^{6} D^{4} a-o^{6} p^{4} pp[44] 1-176
2. a-q^{6} pp[2] 3-191
3. a-h^{6} i^{8} k-z, Aa^{6} Bb-Cc^{8} Dd-ff^{6} pp[2] 3-366
(Book 3 prefaced by Life of Ambrose by Johannes Colterius)
Binding Old. 449 on modern board, repaired. 337x220
6.2 4. a-z, A-Z, Aa-Dd^{6} Ee^{8} Ff-Pp^{6} Qq-Rr^{8} pp[2] 3-366

5. a-z, A-P, A-M^6 pp[2] 1-455
Adams A941 is earlier edition 1555 with same collation.
Rebound in calf. 337x220

ANDRADA, Diego de Payva de, the Elder (1528-1575)

7 Defensio Tridentinae fidei catholicae et integerrimae quinque libris comprehensa.
Ingolstadii, apud Dauidem Sartorium, 1580 8°
*, **, A-Z, a-z, aa-ss^8 ff[16] 1-500 [12]
Adams A1024
MS notes in Latin on front end paper.
Calf on board, repaired. Chain scars. 156x103

8 Orthodoxarum explicationem libri decem.
Venetiis. apud Nicolaum Morettum, 1592 4°
*^{4} B-Z, Aa-Zz, 3A-3Z, 4A-4P^4 4Q^2 ff[4] 5-331 [11]
Adams A1027 has same collation but different imprint and date.
Registrum begins *^{10} A^4 but otherwise agrees.
Fore-edge wrongly marked DIEZ.
Calf on board, repaired. 211x148

ANDREWS, Lancelot, Bishop of Winchester (1555-1626)

9 The forme of consecration of a church or chappel, and of the place of Christian burial.
[London, T. Garthwait, 1668] 12mo
A-C^{12} D^6 pp[2] 1-60
Wing^2 A3127
Bound in with SPARROW : A rationale upon the Book of Common Prayer, 1668 (297)

ANGELUS de Clavasio (1411-1495)

10 Summa de casibus conscientiae.
[Rouen. Jean Le Bourgeois, 1495] 4°
[π^8] ✚^{12} a-r, ⁊, ſ, s-z, ꝛ, ⁊, A-X, A-[M]^8 ff[20] I-CCCCLXXX [8]
Imperfect, wants first 8 leaves and all M except M4, M5.
BMC VIII, 394 BL IA.43940
Rebound. 207x140

ANSWER

11 An answer out of the West to a question out of the North.
[London], Printed in the year 1667 4°
A, B^4 (B4 blank) pp 1-15
Wing^2 A3303A
Signed : Ew^d Eastland
Calf on board. 'English Tracts' in gold on spine. 186x141
Also bound in are sixteen other tracts entered separately, in order as below.

1. Some reflections on a discourse, 1668 (279)
2. [TORSHELL, Samuel]. A case of conscience concerning flying..., 1643 (315)
3. [SEYMOUR, Thomas]. The case of Interest, 1673 (290)
4. [RAWORTH, John]. Satisfaction concerning mixt communions unsatisfactory, 1643 (277)
5. GRANTHAM, Thomas. The Seventh-Day-Sabbath, 1667 (156)
6. [HUMFREY, John]. A case of conscience whether... (182)
7. [HAWORTH, William]. The Quaker's Creed, 1679 (169)
8. WILKINS, John. Ecclesiastes, or a discourse, 1646 (337)
9. [LLOYD, William]. A seasonable discourse shewing..., 1673 (222)
10. The Power of the Christ of God, 1641 (275)
11. [BAXTER, Richard]. The judgement of non-conformists, 1676 (31)
12. HUMFREY, John. The Healing Paper, 1678 (183)
13. Tyth Gatherers no Gospel Officers, 1646 (318)
14. [JOHNSON, Robert]. The Gospell and his Maintenance, 1633 (191)
15. [CLARK, Samuel, (of St. Bennet Fink)]. An item against sacriledge, 1653 (85)
16. MEENE, Joshua. A liberall maintenance, 1638 (235)

ANSWER to Several

12 An answer to Several Remarks upon Dr. Henry More his exposition of the Apocalypse and Daniel...

by S.E., Mennonite, & published in English by the Answerer.
London, printed by Miles Flesher for Walter Kettilby, 1684 4°
A, b-c (c3 blank, -c4), A-Z, Aa-Zz, 3A-3F^{4} pp[22] 1-413
Wing^{2} A3379
The Several Remarks... by S.E. is not in Wing^{2}
Repaired. Chained. 210x137

ANTONINUS, Saint, FORCIGLIONE (Bishop of Florence, 1389-1459)

13 Historia Venerabilis Antonini.
[Basel, Nicolaus Kesler, 1502] Fol.
In 3 volumes:

13.1 Prima pars
A-B^{6} (B6 blank) C-F^{8} G-Z, Aa-Oo^{6} Pp^{4} ff I-CCXV

13.2 Secunda pars
a-b^{6} c^{8} d-r,ꝛ,ſ , s-v, u-z,⁊,ꝯ,ꝝ, aA-nN^{6} ff I-CCXL
Imperfect. Quire z is between q and r

13.3 Tertia pars
X^{1} AA^{1} BB^{1} cc-zz,ꝛꝛ,ꝰꝰ,ꝯꝯ, AA-SS^{6} TT^{8} ff I-CCLVI [3]
Text rubricated irregularly in blue and very glossy red
Adams A1207. Collation differs.
Bequeathed by Francis Trigge, 1606
Binding Old. 1078/1080 (variant). 311x211

14 Summa theologica.
[Lyons, Johannes Cleyn, 1516] Fol.
In two parts (out of four):
1. a-x^{8} no page numbering
2. aa-xx, AA-FF^{8} (FF8 blank) no page numbering
Adams A1217
Bound light calf by Garrett Godfrey, with initials G.G. Old 561. Repaired, 305x204

APULEIUS PLATONICUS (Apuleius Barbarus) (5th century)
De herbarum virtutibus
See under GALEN : De plenitudine, 1528 (151)

AQUINAS, THOMAS, Saint(1224-1274)

15 .....Enarrationes, quas cathenam vere auream dicunt, in quatuor Euangelia.
Parisiis, ex officina Iacobi du Puys, 1566 Fol.
a-z, Aa-Tt^{8} Vv^{6} ff 1-338 [3]
Adams A1481
Signed : Liber Francis Trigge
Binding Old. 449 with 450 (R.B.), rebound by HMSO. 349x209

16 In omnes D. Pauli apostoli epistolas commentaria.....
Quibus accessit.....in Epistolas omnes Canonicas
Antuerpiae, apud Petrum Bellerum, 1591 Fol.
*, a-z, Aa-Oo^{8} ff[8] 1-296
f295 is numbered 299
Adams A1493
Rebound. 393x252

17 Postilla seu expositio in librum Geneseos.
Antuerpiae, in aedibus viduae & haeredum Ioannis Stelsij, 1573 8°
*^{8} A^{4} B-X^{8} Y^{4} ff[8] 1-167 [2?]
Adams A1465
Repaired calf on board. 180x115

18 Summa theologiae in tres partes. Editio novissima.
Coloniae Agrippinae, sumptibus Antonii Hierati, 1622 Fol.
One volume in 5 parts:
1. Prima pars
A-S^{6} pp[12] 1-216

2. Prima secundae partis
**^{4} a-t^6 [-t6 blank] pp[8] 1-220
3. Secunda secundae partis
†^{8} (†1 blank) Aa-Zz, Aaa-Eee^6 Fff^4 [-Fff4, blank] pp[14] 1-341
4. Tertia pars
Ggg-Zzz^6 Aaaa^8 pp[12] 1-208
5. Supplementum ad tertiam partem
AA-PP^6 QQ^4 a-p^6 pp 1-184 [156] [24]
o-p^6 is Augustini Hunnae de sacramentis axiomata.
Signed : Edoardus Wethered May 29 1632
A. Scarr Anno Domini 30-11-9-7-12-18
Rebound. 310x216

ARETIUS, Benedictus (1505-1574)

19 Problemata theologica continentia praecipuos Christianae religionis locos.....
Lausannae, excudebat Franciscus le Preux, 1578 Fol.
In three parts:
1. ¶-¶¶^{4} (¶4 blank) a-s^6 ff[8] 1-108
2. a-r^6 s^4 ff 1-103 [1]
Imperfect. Wants h2, h5
3. A-O^6 ff 1-84
Adams A1618
Tooled calf on oak, Chained. 328x220

20 Theologiae problemata... Editio nova.
[Geneva, Johannes le Preux, 1617] Fol.
¶^{4} A-Z, Aa-Zz, Aaa, Bbb^6 Cccc^8 ff[4] cols. 1-1120 ff[13]
Imperfect, wants ¶1
NA 0386202
Calf on oak, repaired. Chained. 328x200

ARIAS, Benedictus (MONTANUS) (1527-1598)

21 Commentaria in duodecim prophetas : nunc tandem ab ipso auctore recognita.
Antuerpiae, Christophori Plantini, 1583 4°
π^4 A-Z, a-z, AA-EE^8 FF^{10} GG-II^8 KK^4 pp[8] 1-888
Adams M1633
Calf on board. 255x180

ARNOBIUS, Iunioris (and ARNOBIUS, Afer) (fl. 460)

22 D. Arnobi Afri [actually Iunioris] vetusti pariter ac laudatissimi scriptoris commentarij pij iuxta ad eruditi in omnes Psalmos [edited D. Erasmus].
Euisdem [actually Arnobius Afer] disputationum adversus gentes libri VIII.
Basileae, (H. Froben and N. Episcopus), 1560 8°
a-z, A-Z, Aa-Gg^8 pp[34] 1-789 [24]
Adams A2000
On title page: Grantham Library [in hand of Jo: Harrison, Vicar, 1710-36].
Back end paper MS in Latin, in 16th century hand.
Repaired. Chain scars. 168x113

ATHANASIUS, Saint (Bishop of Alexandria, c.296-373)

23 Omnia quae extant opera.
Parisiis, apud Michaelem Sonnium, 1581 Fol.
ã^6 a-z, A-Z, Aa-Tt^6 Vu^4 (Vu4 blank) pp[12] 1-670 [86]
Adams A2086
Calf on board, repaired, Chain scars. 344x244

AUGUSTINE, Saint (Bishop of Hippo, 354-430)

24 [Opera omnia]
Basileae, ex officina Frobeniana, 1569 Fol.
Ten tomes bound as five volumes (four extant):
24.1 Tom.I Retractionum (et) confessionum.....
A-D^6 E$^{4-1}$ a-z, A-O^6 (O6 blank) ff[27] cols. 1-882

Imperfect, wants A1
Tom.II Epistolarum
a-z, A-P^6 ff[1] cols. 5-896 ff[1]
Tom.III Τα διδακτικα
a-z, A-Y^6 ff[1] cols. 5-1078
Rebound, Calf on board. 385x254
24.2 [Presumably Tom.IV, V]. not extant.
24.3 Tom.VI Τα πολεμικα
a-z, A-L^6 MN^8 ff[1] cols. 1-878
Tom.VII Contra Donatistarum
a-z, A-Z, Aa-Oo^6 ff[1] cols. 5-1438
Calf on board, part of original binding Old. 449 by R.B., rebound. 389x255
24.4 Tom.VIII Enarrationes in Psalmos
a-z, A-Z, Aa-Zz, AA-CC^6 DD^8 (DD8 blank) ff[1] cols. 1-1756
Imperfect, wants a1, a2
Tom.IX In Novum Testamentum
a-z, A-Z, Aa-Dd^6 ff[1] cols. 5-1198. cols. 1193, 1194 numbered wrongly
Rebound. 386x255
24.5 Tom.X Sermones habet
a-z, A-Z, Aa-Zz, AA-CC^6 BB^8 ff[1] cols. 5-1706
Imperfect, wants a1, a2
Index A-Z, AA-DD^6 EE^8
Original calf on board, **Old.** 449 by R.B. in front, new back cover. 387x255
All volumes Adams A2166

AUGUSTINUS HUNNAE
25 De sacramentis axiomata
(Cologne, Antonius Hieratus, 1622)
See AQUINAS : Summa theologiae, 1622 (18) of which it forms part.

BABINGTON, Gervase (Bishop of Exeter, 1550-1610)
26 A very fruitful exposition of the Commandements by way of questions and answers for greater plainnesse.
London, R. Robinson for Thomas Charde, 1596 4°
*-$***^4$ B-P^8 (P8 verso blank) pp[24] 1-223
STC^2 1098
Bound in with KINGE : Lectures upon Jonas, 1597 (201)

BALBUS, Iohannes (de Ianua) (d.1296)
27 [Summa que Catholicon appellatur.]
[Lugduni, Nicolaus Wolff, 1503] Fol.
a-z, A-O^8 P-Q^6 308 unnumbered leaves
Imperfect, wants a1
Adams B72
Bequeathed Francis Trigge 1606
Calf on board, front board renewed, chain scars, 355x250
Contemporary Cambridge binding, Old. 1017 with 594

BALE, John (Bishop of Ossory, 1495-1563)
28 [Illustrium Maioris Brittaniae scriptorum...summariũ]
[Gippeswici, per Ioannem Ouerton 1548] 4°
[i.e. Weseliae, per Theod. Plateanum, 1549]
A,✠,✠✠, A-Z, Aa-Zz, 3A-$3S^4$ ff[12] 1-255
Imperfect, wants A1, foliation interchanges 248, 251.
Spurious colophon : Gippeswici per Ioannem Ouerton 1548
Roman type but W is black letter throughout.
STC^2 1296 Adams B135
Note on back end paper : This book belongs to Trigge's Library. It has been missing for several years but was recovered by G.G. in 1843.
Binding Old. 857 (G.K.) on board from printers' waste sheets pasted together.
Repaired. 215x158
See W. T. Davies 'A bibliography of John Bale' in Oxford Bibliographic Society

Proc. and Papers V, 1939, pp 201-279

BARONIUS, Caesar (1538-1607)

29 Annales ecclesiatici. Editio postrema.
Moguntiae, typis Balthasaris Lippii, 1601-1603 [1607] Fol.
Ten tomes extant out of twelve, bound in 6 volumes:

29.1 Tomus primus
)(,)()(, A-Z, Aa-Rr, a-d^{6} e^{4} ff[12] cols. 1-966 ff[28]
Tomus secundus
)(^{2} A-Z, Aa-Tt^{6} Vv^{4} a-d^{6} ff[2] cols. 1-1022 ff[24]

29.2 Tomus tertius
A-Z, Aa-Yy^{6} Xx^{4} (Xx4 blank) a-c^{6} d^{8} (d8 blank) ff[6] cols. 1-1042 ff[26]
Tomus quartus
)(, A-Z, Aa-Oo^{6} Pp^{8} a-d^{6} (d6 blank) ff[6] cols. 1-918 ff[24]

29.3 Tomus quintus
)(, A-Z, Aa-Pp^{6} A*-D^{*6} E^{*4} ff[6] cols. 1-962 ff[30]
Tomus sextus
)(, A-Z, Aa-Oo^{6} Pp^{8} Qq-Vv^{6} ff[6] cols. 1-910 ff[30]

29.4 Tomus septimus
)(, A-Z, Aa-Zz^{6} Aaa-Bbb^{6} ff[6] cols. 1-994 ff[12]
Tomus octavus
)(, A-Z, Aa-Ss^{6} Tt^{8} ff[6] cols. 1-908 ff[26]

29.5 Tomus nonus
)o(^{4} A-Z, Aa-Zz, Aaa-Ccc^{6} Dd^{8} ff[4] cols. 1-1144 ff[32]

29.6 Tomus decimus
†^{4} A-Z, Aa-Zz, Aaa^{6} Bbb^{4} , a-d^{6} e^{8} ff[4] cols. 1-1144 ff[32]
Engraved title page for all tomes with slot for printed tome number. Date on title page on tom.X altered to 1603 by addition of II. Engraving of Baronius on †4 of tom.X, dated 1603
All volumes NB 0138132
Bequeathed by Francis Trigge 1606. [Tomus XII not published till 1607, XI published in1605]
Calf on board, blind tooled. 360x331

BASIL, Saint, Bishop of Caesarea in Cappadocia (c.327-379)

30 [Opera....omnia : iam recens per Wolfgangum Musculum parim locis aliquot castigata, parim luculentis accessionibus aucta....Monodia Gregorij Nazianzeni in Magnum Basilium, per Raphaelem Volaterranum conversa.]
[Basiliae, per I.Oporinem et haeredes I. Heruagij, 1565] Fol.
Three books bound as one volume:
1. [α^{8}] a-z, A-Q^{6} R^{8} S^{6} T^{4} pp 1-484 [20]
2. A-Z, Aa-Hh^{6} Ii-Kk^{8} pp 1-388 [16]
Ii3 is signed Hh3 in error
3. AA-ZZ, Aaa-Eee^{6} Fff^{4} Ggg-Ttt^{6} pp 1-491 [12]
Imperfect, wants α^{8}
Adams B341
Front binding Old. 777 on board, back Old. 449, repaired. 331x220

BAXTER, Richard (1615-1691)

31 The judgment of Non-conformists of the interest of reason in matters of religion.
London, printed in the year 1676 4°
A-C^{4} pp[2] 1-21
Wing^{2} B1293
Bound in with : An answer out of the West, 1667 (11)

BELLARMINE, Robert (S.J.) (1542-1621)

32 Disputationes de controversus... adversus... haeriticos. Editio tertia.
Ingolstadii, ex officina typographica Davidis Sartorii, 1590-97 Fol.
In three volumes:

32.1 (1590)
*^{4} A^{8} B-L^{6} M^{4} N-Z^{6} a-b^{6} c^{8} d-z^{6} Aa^{8} Bb-Mm^{6} Nn^{8} Oo-Zz, Aaa-Ggg^{6} Hhh^{4} Lll-Mmm^{6} Nnn^{8} Ooo-Zzz, Aaaa-Cccc^{6} Dddd-Ffff^{4} Gggg (-4G6 blank) ff[4] cols. 1-2195 ff[18]
Adams B495

32.2 (1597)
*, **, A-L^{6} M^{4} N-S^{6} T^{8} V-Z, a-Z, Aa-Zz, Aaa-Ccc^{6} Ddd^{8} Fff^{6} Ggg^{8} ff[12] cols. 1-1739 ff[21]
Adams B496

32.3 (1593) (adds 'Oratio in scholis habità')
)(^{6} A, B^{6} C^{4} D-Z^{6} a-z, Aa-Zz (Tt6 blank), Aaa-Ccc^{6} Ddd^{4} ff[6] cols. 1-1515 (+ pp 1516-1526) ff[40]
p 1526 is numbered 5126
Adams B495
Rebound, calf on board. 330x214

BENEVENIUS, Antonius
Libellus de Abditis nonnullis ac mirandis morborum & sanationum causis.
See under GALEN : De plenitudine, 1528 (151)

BERCHORIUS, Petrus (Pierre Bersuire) (1290-1362)

33 [In dictionarum seu morale repertorium.]
[Venetis, apud Gasparem Bindonum, 1598] Fol.
One volume in three parts:
1. *^{8} **^{6} A-Z, AA-KK^{8} pp[28] 1-527
Imperfect, wants *1-3, Y5, Y6, S2-5
2. *, **, ***, A-Z, Aa-Qq^{8} Rr^{10} pp[48] 1-653
3. †, ††^{8} †††^{6} A-Z, Aa-Hh^{8} Ii^{6} (-Ii6 blank) pp[44] 1-506
Adams B809
Calf on oak, not in Oldham but roll type F, rebound. Chained. 341x229

34 [Reductorii moralis libri quatordecim.]
[Venetis, apud Gasparem Bindonum, 1589] Fol.
*^{4} A-Z, Aa-Vu^{8} Xx^{6} pp[4] 1-698
Imperfect, wants *4
Adams B816
Also bound in : Reductorium super totam Bibliam, 1589 (35)
Calf on oak, damaged by chain. 336x213
Binding not in Oldham (Roll type FI)

35 Reductorium morale super totam Bibliam,
Venetis, apud Gasparem Bindonum, 1589 Fol.
†, A-R^{8} S^{6} pp[16] 1-283
Adams B815
Bound in with his Reductorii moralis, 1589 (34)

BERNARD, Saint (Abbot of Clairvaux) (1090-1153)

36 Opera omnia.
Paris, 1586 Fol.
(Privilege to Jacques du Puis, Sebastian Nivelle and Michel Sonnius)
Device of Great Ship and arms of Paris (see also CHRYSOSTOM : Opera (83))
Two tomes bound together:
Tom.I ã^{8} a-z, aa-zz, A-Z, AA-DD^{6} EE^{8} FF^{6} ff[8] cols. 1-1794
FF4 is blank, FF5 is title page to Tom.II, FF6 blank.
Tom.II a-z, A-X, a-o^{6} (M, N upper case) p^{4} A^{6} cols. 1-1046 ff[94]
Adams B714
Binding Old. 449 on oak board. (R.B.). 422x269

BEZA, Theodorus Vezelius (1519-1605)

37 In historiam Passionis et sepulturae Domini Nostri Iesu Christi. Homilae ex Gallicis latinae factae.
[Geneva] Joannes le Preux 1592 8°
¶^{8} a-z, A-Z, Aa-Qq^{8} (Qq7.8 blank) pp[16] 1-953 [36]
Adams B923
Calf on board. Chain removed. 174x106

38 Tractatus theologicarum. Secunda editio.
[Geneva] Eustathius Vignon, 1582 Fol.
Three volumes bound together:
I. α^{4} β^{6} a-k^{6} l-m^{4} n-z, A-Z, Aa-Mm^{6} Nn^{4} ¶^{6} pp[20] 1-694 [15]

Imperfect, wants α4
Adams B955

II ¶ ² a-z, A-F⁶G⁸ *⁴ pp[4] 1-363 [7]
Adams B958

III *⁴ Aa-Zz, Aaa-Kkk⁶ Lll-Ppp⁴ Q⁶ Rrr, Sss⁴ p[4] p[4] 1-447 [16]
Adams 959

Binding Old. 436 with 973 (Reynes), repaired. Chained. 356x238

BIBLE (POLYGLOT)

39 Biblia Sacra hebraice chaldaice graece & latine. [Ed. Benedictus Arias Montanus] (accesserunt) Testamentum Novum syriace graece & latine... Apparatus Bibliorum.
[Antwerp, Christopher Plantin, 1569-73] Fol.
Vols. II, III, IV only out of eight.
Vol. II in two parts:

39.1 1. (Joshua - II Kings)
π⁴ A-Z, a-z, Aa-Qq⁶ pp[9] 2-720

2. (Chronicles I and II)
A-S⁶ (S6 blank) pp[1] 2-213 [3]

Vol.III in two parts

39.2 1. (Esdras I Nehemiah [Esdras II])
π² A-G⁶ pp[3] 4-83

1a. (Esdras III and IV, Tobias, Judith, Esther - Song of Songs)
iiG⁸ iiiG⁶ H-Z, Aa-Zz, aA-kK⁶ lL⁴ pp[28] 73-679

Imperfect, wants Rr, Esdras III and IV is 14 leaves not numbered, H1 is p 73

2. (Wisdom, Ecclesiasticus)
a-l⁶ (l6 blank) pp[1] 2-130

Volume as now bound contains only parts 1 and 2.
Part 1a is broken into fragments at present loose in a cover, but is complete except for Rr (Psalms 105-107)

39.3 Vol. IV in two parts:

1. (Isaiah - Malachi)
π² A-Z, a-z, Aa-Zz, AA-GG⁶HH⁴ pp[3] 4-919

2. (Maccabees I and II)
a-k⁶ l⁴ pp 1-128

The catalogus librorum of 1608 lists all eight volumes as extant but there is no trace of the missing five, even as fragments.
Calf on board, rebound. 438x290
B.Street: Historical Notes of Grantham (1857), p.157, states that the Antwerp Polyglot was presented by Bishop Sanderson in 1661, and the Benefactions Board now in the bellringing chamber records his gift of a Polyqlot Bible. Since Sanderson, while Rector of Boothby Pagnell, is known to have worked with Brian Walton in the compilation of the London Polyglott (6 volumes, 1654-1657) it is possible that he had borrowed the rare and not easily obtainable volumes from St Wulfram's Church. When he became Bishop of Lincoln in 1660 and returned the books, they may well have been recorded as a gift. If indeed only three of the eight volumes were returned this would explain the missing group of five titles in the Catalogus, which elsewhere has only unassociated items missing.

40 Novum Testamentum Graecum cum vulgata interpretatione Latine Graeci contextus lineas inserta... Ed. B. Arias Montanus.
Accesserunt Apocryphi libri
Antuerpiae, ex officina Christophori Plantini, 1584
In two parts:

1. Novum Testamentum
¶ ⁴ A-Y⁶ Z⁶ pp[8] [1] 2-186

2. Bibliorum Pars quae Hebraice non invenitur
Aa-Qq⁴ pp 1-128

Also part of volume but separately printed.
Biblia Hebraica eorundem Latina interpretario Xantis Pagnini Lucensis [Ed. B. Arias Montanus].
Antuerpiae, ex officina Christophori Plantini, 1584
In four parts:

1. † ⁴†† ,A-O⁶ p⁸ pp[20] 1-183
2 a-x⁶ y-z⁸ pp 1-283
3. aa-gg⁶ pp 1-84

4. AA-RR^6 pp 1-203
(Signatures read from right to left and text is paginated to follow the Hebrew)
Adams B972
Calf on board. Chained. 364x219

BIBLE (BIBLIA LATINA)

41. Textus Biblie cũ glosa ordinaria/Nicolai de lyra postilla/moralitatibus eiusdem/Pauli Burgesis additiõibus/Matthie Thoring replicis.
[Basel, Johann Froben 1507/8] Fol.
In 7 volumes:

41.1 Pars prima: Genesis - Deuteronomius
a-z, A$^{8.6}$ B-C^6 D-Z, aa-ff$^{8.6}$ gg-hh^8 ff 1-377
Front, new calf on oak board, back Old. 436 with 973 (Reynes) on oak. f183 torn.
Signed : F. Wright 1597 Febr 3

41.2 Pars secunda: losue - Hester
a-d^8 e-f^6 g-q^8 r-v$^{8.6}$ x^6 y-z, A-B^8 C^6 D-P$^{8.6}$ Q-S^6 T-Y^8 ff 1-315
Signed : F. Wright 1596 Prys vis viii d
End paper pastedowns are uncut unfolded half sheets (sig. civ) of an octavo service book, [Missale ad usum Sarum, Johannes Hamman (or Hertzog) Venice, for F Egmont, London, 1494. STC^2 16168]
Binding Old. 436 with 975 on oak board. Chained.

41.3 Pars tertia: Iob-Ecclesiasticum in se cõtinẽs glosam ordinariã cũ expositione lyre litterali et morali: necnõ additionibus ac replicis
a-t$^{8.6}$ v^4 x-z, A-Z, aa-qq$^{8.6}$ rr^6 ff 1-440
Signed : F. Wright
Rebound, original cover on back, Old. 436 with 973 (Reynes).

41.4 Quarta pars: Esaie - Machabeorum
a-z, A-Z, aa-vv$^{8.6}$ xx^8 yy^{10} ff 1-479
Ad lectores dated Basel 1507, (21June)
Binding Old. 436 with 973 on oak, Chained.

41.5 (Quinta pars: Mattheus - Iohannes)
a-z, A-M$^{8.6}$ ff[2] 3-244
Imperfect...wants a1, a2.
Front pastedown is sig. h2 from Sarum Missal (see 41.2)
Binding Old. 436 with 973 oak, repaired. Chained.

41.6 Sexta pars biblie cũ glosa ordinaria et expositiõe lyre litterali morali: necnõ additiõib⁹ ac replicis.
Romanes-Apocalypsin.
[a-z, A-R$^{6.8}$ S^6] ff 1-286
Ad lectores on S6 recto (not in vols. 1-5) gives Basel, Froben, 1508, 3 March
Note: f286 line 1 ends...qui omni cu - (see 42)
Signed : Wilhelmo Welles pertinet hic Liber. ps vis
Modern calf on oak boards.
Aberrant binding with gatherings in order a-o, y, c, t-x, q-r, z-B, P, S, D to end.

41.7 Repertorium alphabeti cũ sententiarũ prestantiũ cõtẽtinũ...
a^8 b-z, A-N^6 no foliation. [218 leaves]
Ad lectores dated 'ex valle Engadi...1508 VIII kale Novebris'
Binding Old.436 with 973, repaired.
Complete set Adams B985.
All volumes 360x240

Another edition, Volume 6 only

42 Textus Biblie pars sexta Romanos-Apocalypsin.
(Basel, Johann Froben, 1508, 3rd March) Fol.
aa-zz, AA-RR$^{8.6}$ SS^6 ff 1-286
Not the same setting as 41.6.
Catchwords identical but line endings differ.
Woodcut initials different throughout.
f 286 line 1 ends.....qui omni (see 41.6)
Not in Adams or BL.
Binding Old.703 with 997. 358x246

BIBLE (BIBLIA LATINA)

43 [Testamenti veteris biblia sacra quibus etiam adiunximus noui testamenti libros. Tr. ab I. Tremillio et F Iunio.]
[Londoni, Gul.N[orton], 1592-93] Fol.
Volume in six parts:
1. Geneseos - Deuteronomii
[?]A-P^6 pp(sic) 177
Imperfect, wants A1 and preliminaries.
2. Iehoschuhiae - Estherae
Aa-Ss^6 ff 104
3. Iobi - Libri canticorum
Aaa-Mmm^6 Nnn^4 ff 76
4. Ieschahae - Maleaci
Aaaa-$Yyyy^6$ $Xxxx^4$ ff 128
5. Libri apocryphi (tr. ab F Iunio)
Aaaaa-$Lllll^6$ $Mmmmm^8$ ff 74
6. Testamentum novum sive foedus novum è graeco archetypo, Latino sermone redditum, Theodoro Beza interprete
[A]-$[Kk]^6$ $[Li]^4$ (brackets in signatures) ff 198
STC^2 2061
Calf on board, wrongly marked 'Vulgate' on fore-edge. 293x193

BIBLE, N.T. POLYGOT

44 [Testamentum nouum [graecum] : interpretationes duae : vna, vetus : altera, T.Bezae, nunc quarto recognita.]
[Geneva, Henricus Stephanus II, 1588] Fol.
In two parts:
1. $¶^6$ A-Z^6 Aa-Yy^6 Zz^8 α^8 pp[10] 1-555 [32]
2. a-z^6 aa-tt^6 vv^8 xx-yy^6 pp 1-519 [24]
Imperfect, wants ¶1-2
Adams B1711
Calf on board. 350x217

BIBLE (Genesis)

45 Genesis cum catholica expositione ecclesiastica
[by eleven authors, including Luther]
Morgiis, sumptibus Ioannis Le Preux & Eustathii Vignon, 1585 Fol.
$¶^4$ a-z, A-V^4 X^6 (-X6 blank) pp[8] 1-353
Adams B1312
Calf on board. 380x238

BIBLE (English)

46 The New Testament of our Lord Jesus Christ.... translated out of the Greek by Theod. Beza.....
Englished by L.Tomson
London, deputies of Christopher Barker, 1595 Fol.
4M-4Z, 5A-$5M^6$ $5N^4$ ff 488-627
STC^2 2165 (N.T. only)
Title page is a facsimile.
Bookplate Gregory, signed : Henry Gregory, 18 Mecklenburgh Square
Given by E.M.Tenison to W.Stanhope Lovell in 1930 and by him to Grantham in 1944.
Early 19th century calf, now denatured and covers broken away. 275x191

47 The Bible, that is, the holy scriptures conteined in the Old and New Testaments. Translated according to the Ebrew and Greek. [Geneva version or 'Breeches' Bible]
London, Christopher Barker, 1599 4^0
[Amsterdam, J. Stam, 1640?]
In three parts:
1. $¶^4$ A-Z^8 $\&^6$ ff[4] 1-190
2. Aa-Qq^8 (Qq8 blank) ff[1] 2-127
Two title pages. The first title is in heart-shaped compartment with vignettes of tribes, apostles and evangelists. Woodcut maps and vignettes.
3. New testament (Engelished by L.Tompson)

Aaa-Qqq^8 Rrr^4 ff[2] 3-121 [10]
STC^2 2174 (Esther 1, 1 has 'seven and/ twenty provinces'. Revelation is in Junius version)
Presented to A. Bousted 1891, and by him in 1931.
Also bound in : The Psalmes of David in Meeter, 1650 (53)
Brown calf on board, originally gold tooled, marbled end papers. 219x169

48 [Authorized Version], with Apocrypha
London, Bonham Norton and John Bill 1619 4^0
¶^{8} (+ 3 leaves) A-Z, Aa-Zz, 3A-3L^8 Mmm^4 pp[16] [6] 1-730 [2] 738-918
STC^2 2253 (Ruth 3,15 reads 'he')
Title page of woodcut vignettes as Bible (Barker 1599) (47)
Pasted in after ¶, three leaves only A1, F1/2 of The genealogies recorded in the sacred scriptures ... by J.S
No imprint (see SPEED, John)
Leaf Zz6 is title page of New Testament with imprint: Printed by the Printers to the University of Cambridge 1630. (Not in STC) On its verso is pasted a Norton and Bill title page dated 1620.
Signed : John Wing 1710, with notes by William Rogers Saxilby 1817.
Vellum on board, marbled end papers, well used. 220x168

49 [Authorized version]
(London. Robert Barker and assignes of John Bill, 1634) 4^0
a-z, Aa-Zz, 3A-3K^8 3L^6 pp 1-718 [2] 721-904
STC 2313 (p3 headline is Adams genealogies)
Wants t.p. but N.T. has its own title page Yy6 with woodcut vignettes as Bible (Barker 1599 (47)) and Bible (Norton and Bill, 1619 (48))
Bound in with : The Book of Common Prayer, 1634 (see LITURGY) (216)

50 [Authorized version]
London, assigns of J. Bill, T. Newcombe and Henry Hills, 1681 12mo
A-Z, Aa-Zz, Aaa-Ddd^{12} no pagination
Wing^2 B2317
Also bound in : The Whole book of Psalms (Sternhold and Hopkins), 1682 (304)
Red rules throughout inserted by hand.
Black calf on board with silver mounts and clasps.
Nameplate engraved 'Nicholas Knight'. 115x62
Presented by Lillian Scott 1950

51 [Authorized version ('Vinegar' Bible)]
Oxford, John Baskett 1716-17 Fol.
One volume in two parts, imperial folio:
1. Old Testament 1717
π^2 *1 a, b, c^2 *2, A-4P^6 4Q^4 (Q4 title leaf of Pt II) leaves not numerated [10 + 512]
2. New Testament 1716
(Q4) A-X^6 Y^4 leaves not numerated [1 + 130]
Frontispiece, steel engraving after Thornhill, other plates as vignettes at beginning and ending of principal books. Marginal notes and text columns enclosed in red rules inserted by hand. Misprint 'vinegar' for 'vineyard' on column heading for Luke XX.
Black calf on board, gold tooling, edges gilt, marbled end papers in two pieces. 564x364
Presented by Canon C.W. Foster in 1936.

52 [Authorized version]
The Royal Universal Family Bible or, a complete library of Divine Knowledge...with practical reflection: on each chapter...by the Reverend John Herries
London, for Fielding and Walker, 1780 Fol.
In two parts:
1. X^6 B-Z, Aa-Zz, 3A-6Z^2 A-7U^2
2. B-Z, Aa-Zz, 3A-6Z, 7A-7C^2
No pagination. 100 Plates individually dedicated with printed direction to binder for insertion.
Presented by John Cheshire 1948. Front paste down signed : John Adnall his book, 1783, Sturton, Nottinghamshire.
Brown doeskin on board, gold spine label, HERRIES BIBLE.

BIBLE (Psalms)

53 The Psalmes of David in Meeter, newly translated.....
Allowed by the authority of the Generall Assembly of the Kirk of Scotland.
Edinburgh, Evan Tyler, 1650 4°
A-P^{2} (-P2 blank) ff[29]
Wing^{2} B2441
Pages originally numbered, but trimmed to fit Bible.
Bound in with : BIBLE, Barker 1599 (47)
See also STERNHOLD and HOPKINS

BONAVENTURUS, Saint (c.1217-1274)

54 [In secundũ Lucam evãgelium commentarij]
Antuerpiae, apud Gregoriũ Bontiũ, (excudebat Joannes Crinitus, 1539) 8^{0}
One volume in two parts:
1. ❧^{8} ¶¶^{6} A-Z, Aa-Pp^{8} pp[28] 1-607
Imperfect, wants ❧1
2. AA-ZZ, AAa-GGg^{8} [+1] pp 1-483 [1]
Adams B2409
Calf on board, repaired, blind stamped with medallions not in Oldham. Chained. 177x107

BRANDMYLLERUS, Joann (1533-1596)

55 Conciones funebres CLXXX.
Hanoviae, impensis Claudij Marnij & haeredum Joannis Aubrij, 1603 8^{0}
A-Z, Aa-Xx^{8} pp 1-676 [20]
BL copy is 846.i.21
Bound in with his Conciones nuptiales, 1603 (56)

56 Conciones nuptiales XL ex Vetere Testamente et XX ex Novo.....
Hanoviae, impensis Claudij Marnij & haeredum Joannis Aubrij, 1603 8^{0}
A-Z, Aa-Dd^{8} pp[2] 3-405 [26]
Not in BL or NUC
Calf on board, repaired. 164x99
Also bound in : Conciones Funebres, 1603 (55)

BUCER, Martin (1492-1551)

57 Praelectiones in Epistolam D. Pauli ad Ephesios,
Basiliae, apud Petrum Pernam, 1562 Fol.
a-r^{6} (r6 blank) pp 1-190 [12]
Adams B3046
Bound in with his Metaphrases et Enarrationes..., 1536 (59)

58 In sacra quatuor euãgelica, enarrationes perpetuae.
[Geneuae] Oliua Roberti Stephani, 1553 Fol.
*, A-Z, A-Q^{8} R^{10} pp[16] 1-311 [22]
Adams B3041
Bound in with his Psalmorum libri quinque, 1554 (60)

59 Metaphrases et enarrationes perpetuae epistolarum D. Pauli apostoli... tomus primus - in epistolam ad Romanos
Argentorati, per VVendelinum Rihelium, 1536, Fol.
*^{6} a, b^{6} c, d^{4} e-z, A-L^{6} M^{4} N-P^{6} Q-S^{4} T, V^{6} X, Y^{4} pp[12] 1-507
Adams B3043
Also bound in : In Epistolam D. Pauli ad Ephesos, 1562 (57)
Binding Old. 449 (R.B.), repaired. Chain scars. 311x194

60 Psalmorum libri quinque ad Hebraicam veritatem traducti.
[Geneuae] Oliua Roberti Stephani, 1554 Fol.
*, a-z, A-P^{8} pp[16] 1-584 [22]
Also bound in : In sacra quatuor euangeliae, enarrationes perpetuae, 1553 (58)
Calf on board, repaired. Chain scars. 347x238

BULLINGER, Heinrich (1504-1575)

61 Daniel sapientissimus Dei propheta expositus.
homiliis LXVI.... accessit... Epitome temporum.
Tiguri, excudebat Christophorus Froschouerus, 1576 Fol.
In two parts:
1. aa, bb, a-y^6 z^8 ff[12] 1-140
2. Epitome temporum
A-S^6 T^8 ff 1-116
Adams B3218
Calf on board. 325x207
End paper sewn with slips of rubricated manuscript.

62 Ieremais fidelissimus et laboriosissimus Dei propheta expositus concinionibus CLXX.
(accessit) Threnorum seu Lamentationem.
Tiguri, excudebat Christophorus Froschouerus, 1575 Fol.
*, a-z, A-Z, Aa-Ee^6 Ff^4 Gg^6 ff[6] 1-312 [4]
Adams B3215
Calf on oak boards. 293x203
Also bound in : Altercatio synagogae et ecclesiae, 1587 (5)

CALVIN, Jean (1509-1564)

63 Commentarii in Isaiam prophetam. Primum collecti opera & diligentia N. Galisii.
[Geneuae], excudebat Eustathius Vignon, 1583 Fol.
$*^4$ $**^2$ a-z, A-Z^6 Aa-Bb^4 pp[12] 1-530 [25]
Adams B1587. Signatures **1, 2 on slips pasted over errors, but **2 is torn off.
Calf on board, Repaired. 324x206

64 Commentarii integri in Acta Apostolorum
Geneuae, excudebat Eustathius Vignon, 1584 Fol.
$*^4$ a-z, A-F^8 G^4 pp[10] 1-258 [26]
Adams C317
Bound in with his Harmonia ex evangelistis tribus, 1595 (66)

65 Commentarius in librum Psalmorum.
Geneuae, apud Eustathium Vignon, 1578 Fol.
$¶^4$ a-z, A-T^8 V^6 X^4 pp[8] 1-676 [18]
Adams C291 (rabbit in headpiece on ¶ 2)
Contains Psalms in Latin and Hebrew in parallel half columns with commentaries across page below them.
Calf on board, repaired. 319x205

66 Harmonia ex evangelistis tribus composita....
Eiusdem in Iohannem evangelistam commentarius.
Geneuae, apud haeredes Eustathii Vignon, 1595 Fol.
In two parts:
1. Harmonia
$(:)^4$ a-z, aa-gg^6 hh-mm^4 pp[8] 1-376 [24]
2. In Iohannem
A-M^6 N^4 O-R^6 S^4 (S4 blank) pp[4] 5-210
Adams C353. Collation differs.
Rebound. 336x212
Also bound in : Commentarii in Acta Apostolorum, 1584 (64)

67 In omnes Pauli Apostoli epistolas [et] in omnes epistolas canonicas.
Geneuae, apud Eustathium Vignon, 1580 Fol.
In two parts:
1. $*^4$ a-z, A-Z, Aa-Gg^6 Hh^8 pp[8] 1-624 [28]
wants N1
2. A-L^6 pp 1-116 [14]
wants E3
Adams C323
Binding Old. 449 (R.B.) on board, repaired. Chain scars. 333x205

68 In quinque libros Mosis commentarii.
Eiusdem Caluini in librum Iosue commentarius.
[Geneuae], in officina Sanctandreana, 1595 Fol.
In three parts:
1. *, a-z, A-C^6 D^4 pp[12] 1-320
wants b3-b6
2. aa-zz, AA-ZZ, AAA-EEE^6 FFF^4 pp 1-594 [25]
3. A-G^6 (G6 blank) pp 1-79 [2]
Adams C278, part 3 is Adams C282
Old. 449 (R.B) on board, repaired. 325x206

69 Praelectiones in duodecim prophetas (quos vocant) minores.
Geneuae, apud Eustathium Vignon, 1581 Fol.
$¶^6$ a-o p^4 q-z, A-Z, Aa-Vv^6 Xx^4 Yy-Zz^6 AA^4 pp 1-776 [32]
Adams C305
Calf on board. Formerly chained. 330x206

70 Praelectiones in Ezechielis prophetae viginti capita priora....
[Geneuae], apud Petrum Sanctandreanum, 1583 Fol.
$*^4$ A-V^6 X-Y^4 Z^6 ff[4] 1-128 [6]
Adams C301
Rebound. 308x201
Also bound in : Praelectiones in Danielis, 1561 (71)

71 Praelectiones in librum prophetiarum Danielis... Additus est è regione versionis Latinae, Hebraicus & Chaldaicus textus.
Geneuae (excudebat Joannes Laonius) 1561 Fol.
$*^8$ a-z, Aa-Ee^6 Ff^4 ff[8] 1-170 [1]
Adams B1605. Collation differs ff 3, 4 are numbered 5, 6
Bound in with his Praelections in Ezechielis, 1583 (70)

72 Praelectiones in librum prophetiarum Ieremiae et Lamentationes. Tertia editio.
Geneuae, apud haered. Eustath. Vignon, 1589 Fol.
¶, a-z, A-Z, Aa-Zz, AA-CC^6 DD, EE^4 FF^6 pp[12] 1-872 [20]
Adams C298
Calf on board, repaired. 321x209

73 [The Sermons of M. John Caluin upon Deuteronomie gathered by D. Raguenier (trans. Arthur Golding)].
[London, H. Middleton for G. Bishop, 1583] Fol.
$¶^6$ A-Z, Aa-Zz, 3A-3Z, 4A-4Z, 5A-$5Y^6$ $*^8$ pp[12] 1-1243[143]
Imperfect, wants ¶1
STC^2 4442 or 4443
Binding Old. 449 (R.B.) on board, repaired. 290x191

74 [Sermons vpon the booke of Job (Tr. Arthur Golding).]
[London, T. Dawson, for G. Bishop and T. Woodcocke. 1579] Fol.
A^4 $*^6$ $**^8$ A-Z, Aa-Zz, 3A-$3C^8$ pp[36] 1-752
Imperfect, wants A1 and Ccc8
STC^2 4446 or 4447.5
Signed :John Bentley his Booke May 20 1693
Will Higginbotham his book 1683
James Higginbotham 1704 and 1707
Marginalia in English.
Calf on oak, repaired with small tacks. 348x233
Binding Old. 751
74a [Another copy of the above]
Imperfect, wants preliminaries, pp 1-4 and Bbb-Ccc^8
Binding Old. 46 (946) on oak, repaired. 340x219

75 Tractatus theologici omnes...Altera editio... cui accesserunt eiusdem Calvini in libros Senecae de Clementia commentarij
Geneuae, apud Petrum Sanctandreum, 1597 Fol.
In two parts:
1. Tractatus theoligici
¶ , A-Z, AA-ZZ, 3A-4O^6 4p^4 pp[12] 1-1003
2. In libros Senecae de Clementia
a-e^6 f^8 pp 1-75
Adams C384
Binding Old. 449 on board, repaired. Chain scars. 339x203

CASTRO, Alphonsus de (1495-1558)
76 (Aduersus omnes haereses)
([Paris]: Jodocus Badius and Jean Roigny, 1534) Fol.
ã^6 ẽ^4 a-z, A-B^8 C-D^6 ff[10] I-CCXII
Imperfect, wants ã1 and D6
Adams C963
Calf on board, repaired. Chained. 350x219

CELSUS, Aulus Cornelius (c.25 B.C.E. - 50 C.E.)
77 [De re medicâ libri octo....Accessit...liber Scribonii Largi titulo compositionu medicamentorum.]
[Parisiis, apud Christianum Vuechel, (excud. Simon Siluius, 1528)] Fol.
In two parts:
1. De Medicâ
A-B^6 C^8 A-X^6 Y^2 (+ blank) ff[20] 1-128
2. De compositionibus medicamentorum [by Scribonius Largus]
*^{6} **^{4} (**4 blank) Aa-Ff^6 ff[10] 1-31 [5]
Adams C1243. Collation differs for Part 1.
Wants t.p. A1. Four unnumbered leaves at end are letter to Vicianus with verses enumerating drugs in hexameters.
Binding Old. 892 on board, repaired. Chained. 292x209
Back end paper has medical notes in early 16th century hand, and gives English names for herbs.
Also bound in GALEN : De plenitudine [with tracts by others], 1528 (151)

CHAMIER, Daniel (1565-1621)
78 Panstratiae catholicae, sive controversiarum de religione adversus pontificios corpus, tomis quatuor distributum
Geneuae, Typis Roverianis, 1626 Fol.
In four volumes:
78.1 De Canone
(a) † , †† , A-Z, Aa-Zz, Aaa-Ccc^6 Ddd^8 ¶ ^{6} ¶¶ ^{8} pp[36] 1-603 [28]
78.2 De Deo et Dei cultu
π1, a^4 π2 (blank) A-Z, AA-ZZ, 3A-3Z, 4A-4D^6 Eeee^8 ¶, ¶¶^{6}¶¶¶^{8} pp[4] 1-889 [40]
78.3 De Homine
π1, ()^4 π2 (blank) a-z, aa-zz, 3a-3z, 4a-4z, 5a-5l^6 5m^4 † , 2† , 3† , 4† ^{6} 5† ^{4} (5† 4 blank)
pp[4] 1-1247 [54]
78.4 De Sacramentis
π1, a^2 π2 (blank) A-Z, Aa-Zz, 3A-3M ,§ ,§§ ,§§§^{6} (§§§ 6 blank) pp[2] 1-696 [34]
NC 0290031
All volumes calf on board (with end papers from 4° Prayer Book, London, Norton and Bill, 1626).
345x216

79 Another edition of the above.
[Frankfurt] 1627? Fol.
Two volumes only of four, bound as one:
1. Tomus primus - De canone
a-c^4 d^6 AA-ZZ, AAA-BBB^6 (BBB6 blank) pp[36] 1-178
Imperfect, wants a1
2. Tomus secundus. De Deo et Dei Cultu....
):(- 4):(^{4} aA-zZ, aaA-ooO^6 ppP^4 pp[32] 1-452
NC 0290033
Calf on board, repaired. Chained. 383x243

CHEMNITIUS, Martinus (1522-1586)

80 Examinis Concilii Tridenti....in quibis totius doctrinae papisticae firma et solida refutatio.
Francofurti ad Moenum (per Petrum Fabricium), 1585 Fol.
In four parts:
1. Prima pars
)(^{8} ( )(8 blank) A-P^8 Q^4 R^6 S^4 (s4 blank) pp[16] 1-188 [20]
2. Secunda pars
()^4 Aa-Xx^6 Yy^8 pp[8] 1-243 [25]
3. Tertia pars
*^{4} A-S^6 T^8 (T8 blank) pp[8] 1-206 [32]
4. Quarta et postrema pars
)(^{4} a-m^6 n^8 o^6 p^8 (p8 blank) pp[8] 1-160 [28]
Adams C1441
Title page in red and black with woodcut of Council in session.
Calf on board, repaired. Chained. 351x223

81 Libri tres Harmoniae Evangelicae...Edita à Polycarpo Lysero, successore, nomine haeredum.
Francoforti ad Moenum, excudebat Ioannis Spies, 1593 4°
Three volumes bound as two:
81.1 1. Liber primus
a-d, A-Z, Aa-Vv^4 pp[32] 1-342
2. Liber secundus
aa-bb, a-Z, Aa-Hh, Ii^4 (-Ii3, 4 blank) pp[32] 1-251
81.2 Liber tertius
A-Z, Aa-Zz, 3A-3Z, 4A-4C^4 pp[32] 1-550 [6]
Not in Adams. This edn. not in BL.
Calf on board, repaired. Vol 1 chained. 212x159

82 Loci theologici quibus et loci communes P Melancthonis explicantur.
Francoforti ad Moenum, excudebat Iohannes Spies, 1594 4°
Three volumes:
82.1 Prima pars locorum theologicorum
a-d, A-Z, Aa-Zz, 3A-3Z, 4A-4V^4 ff[16] 1-285 [1]
82.2 Secunda pars locorum theologicorum
a-c^4 d^2 A-Z, Aa-Zz, 3A-3Z, 4A-4V^4 ff[14] 1-355 [1]
82.3 Tertia pars locorum theologicorum
)(,)()(, A-Z, Aa-Zz, 3A-3Z, 4A-4C^4 (-C3.4 presumed blank) ff[8] 1-287
Folding table inserted after Ppp2
Adams C1444 (collation differs for Tertia pars.)
Calf on board, repaired. Chain scars. 216x159

CHRYSOSTOM, Saint John (c.347-407)

83 Opera.
(Parisiis, excudebat Dionysis Duvallius), 1588 Fol.
Five tomes and index bound as 3 volumes:
83.1 1. Tomus primus
† ^{4} ã^8 ẽ, ĩ, õ, ũ, ãã, a-z^8 A-T^8 pp[8] 1-96, cols. 1-1341
2. Tomus secundus
A-Z, Aa-Rr^8 Ss^6 ff[2] cols. 1-1296
Imperfect, want Ss, Rr4 is signed Qq4
Calf on oak board, Old. 449 (R.B.), repaired.420x269
83.2 1. Tomus tertius
a-n^8 o-q^6 r-z^8 Aa-Cc^8 Dd^{10} ff[2] cols. 1-840
2. Tomus quartus
A-Z, Aa-Zz, Aa-Gg^8 (-Gg8 presumed blank) ff[1] cols. 5-1692
Calf on oak boards, Old. 449 (R.B.), repaired. 420x269
83.3 1. Tomus quintus
a-z, A-Z, Aa-Kk^8 Ll-Mm^6 (Mm6 blank) ff[1] cols. 5-1836
2. Index
a-m^8 n^4 (n4 blank) 99 leaves not numbered
Title pages for all tomes have the Great Ship device with the arms of Paris and legend LVTETIA.
See BERNARD, St : Opera (36)

Calf on oak boards, Old. 449 (R.B.), repaired. 420x269
All volumes Adams C1521

CHRZASTOWSKI, Andrzej (CHRASTORIUS)

84 (Three works in one volume):
Basiliae per Conr. Vualdkirchium, 1593-94 4°
1. Bellum Iesuiticum sive ducentarum & quinque Iesuiticarum contradictionum.
α, β, a-t^4 v^6 (v6 blank) pp[16] 1-161
2. Due libelli de opificio Missae : quorum prior disputationem contra Robertum Bellarminum...continet.
Aa-Zz, AA-XX^4 YY^6 pp[18] 1-328 [20]
3. Praxis de caeremoniis et canone missae disputatio in theses digesta.
Aaa-Ppp^4 (-Ppp3 and 4 presumed blank) pp[10] 1-104 [1]
Adams C1471 (Date on 1 is MDXCIII with an added I)

[CLARKE, Samuel, of St. Bennet Fink] (1589-1682)

85 An item against sacriledge : or sundry queries concerning tithes
London, printed by Abraham Miller for Thomas Underhill, 1653 4°
A^4 pp[2] 1-6
$Wing^2$ C4525
Bound with : An answer out of the west, 1667 (11)

CLEMENT of Alexandria (Titius Flavius Clemens) (Born c.150)

86 Opera
Basiliae, apud Jean Bibelium, 1526 Fol.
In two parts:
1. α, a-y^4 (y4 blank) pp[8] 1-174
Wants α4
Woodcut borders on a1 recto
2. A-M^4 pp 1-83 [13]
Not in Adams, NUC or BL
Also bound in are IRENAEUS : Opus in quinque libros digestum, 1526 (187) and PHILO JUDAEUS Libri antiquitatem..., 1527 (268)
Modern rebinding, original calf Old. 951 with 979 on new oak. End papers are rubricated MS on vellum (13th century). 300x207

87 [Omnia opera (trans. from Greek G. Hervet)]
Florence, Laurentius Torrentius, 1551) Fol.
In three parts:
1. A-D^6 pp[2] 3-46
2. a-i^6 k^4 (k4 blank) pp[2] 3-113
3. $*^2$ aa-zz, Aa-Cc^6 Dd, Ee^4 pp 1-277 [51]
Adams C2105
Part 1 wants A1. Part 2 has Medici device on title page.
Calf on board. 347x224

CULPEPER, Nicholas

see RIVERUS, Lazarus : The practice of physick (tr N. Culpeper).

CYPRIAN, Saint (of Alexandria) (c.380-444)

88 Opera.
Apud Basileam, ex off. Frobeiana, 1521 Fol.
a-z, A-Y^6 Z, Aa^8 pp[12] 1-515 [15]
Adams C3150
Signature printed sideways on z
Binding Old. 991 with 706 on boards. Back end paper rubricated MS on vellum, some marginalia, parchment tags to mark sections. 333x215

CYRIL, Saint (of Alexandria) (c.380-444)

89 Opera omnia.
Parisiis, apud Michaëlem Sonnium, 1573 Fol.
in two parts:
1. Tomus I
†^{4} a-z, A-Y^6 (Y6 blank) pp[8] cols. 1-1074
2. Tomus II
a-z, Aa-Nn^6 Oo^2 (-Oo2 blank?) cols. 4-762
Adams C3170
Calf on board with gold tooling and title on spine.
Chain scars. 387x245

DANAEUS, Lambertus (c.1530-1595)

90 Ad Robert. Bellarmini disputationes theologicas responsio.
Geneuae, apud Ioannem le Preux, 1596 8°
One work bound as two volumes:
90.1 † , †† , ††† (††† 8 blank), a-z, A-Z, Aa-Dd^8 Eel, pp[42] 1-802
Bb and part of Cc signed B, C
90.2 π^2 Ee (Ee1 is in Vol. I) - Zz, AA-ZZ, AAa-EEe^8 FFf^4 GGg^1 (-Gg2 blank?) pp 803-1532 [30]
On π^1 is binder's half title Primae Partis Altera pars
Adams D28. Collation differs.
Repaired. 174x108
90.2a Another copy of Vol. II (same edition)

91 Ad tomum secundem controversiarum Roberti Bellarmini responsio.
Geneuae, excudebat Ioannes le Preux, 1598 8°
*, **, A-Z, Aa-Ss^8 (Ss7.8 blank) pp[32] 1-651
Not in Adams, NUC or BL
Calf on board, repaired. 174x107
Marked 'Grantham Library'

92 Christianae isagoges.
Geneuae, apud Eustathium Vignon,1587-91 8°
Four parts only out of five, bound as two volumes:
92.1 1. Pars prima (1588)
*^{4} A-S^8 T, V^4 ff[4] 1-152
2. Pars altera (1597)
*^{8} a-z, A-N^8 O^4 pp[16] 1-584
Adams D31 (collation differs for Pars prima)
Calf on board. Chain scars. 179x110
92.2 4. Pars quarta (1591)
*^{8} **^{4} a-z, A-S^8 pp[24] 1-656
5. Pars quinta (1588)
*, a-z, A-G^8 ff[8] 1-232
Not in Adams
Marked 'Grantham Library'
Brown calf. 182x111

93 Commentariorum in prophetas minores.
Geneuae, apud Eustathium Vignon, 1586 Fol.
π, ¶ ^{4} a-z, A-Z, Aa-Ss^8 Tt^4 pp[6] 1-1032 [1]
Adams D32
Cloth on board, repaired. 173x108

94 Opuscula omnia theologica.
Geneuae, apud Eustathium Vignon, 1583 Fol.
¶ ^{4} a-z, A-Z, Aa-Zz, AA-ZZ, AAa-ZZz, AAA-ZZZ^6 AAAa^4 pp[8] 1-1625 [39]
As Adams D51, but has GENEVAE printed and wants diagram.
Possibly bequeathed by Francis Trigge
Calf on board, Old. 948, repaired. Chain scars. 364x230

95 Politices Christianae libri septem.

[Geneva], apud haeredes Eustathii Vignon, 1596 8°
¶⁴, A-Z, Aa-Nn⁸ pp[16] 1-576
Adams D58
Back end paper is printed index from another work.
Calf on board. Chain scars. 173x107
'Grantham Library' on title page.

96 Vetustissimarum primi mundi antiquitatum sectiones.
[Geneva], excudebat Ioannes le Preux, 1596 8°
¶ , A-Z, Aa-Ff⁸ (Ff8 blank) pp[16] 1-452 [11]
Adams D68
Inscribed 'Grantham Library' (in hand of John Harrison)
Repaired. 174x108

DIEZ, Phillipus (1550 - c.1601)
97 Concionum quadruplicium libri (altera editio).
Lugduni, apud Petrum Landry,1589 8°
In five volumes:
97.1 Vol. I not extant
97.2 Tomus secundus concionum quadruplicium quae quotidie in septuagesima habentur
[], a-z, A-Z, Aa-Rr⁸ Ss⁴ pp[] 1-940 [72]
Calf on board. 173x105
97.3 Tomus tertius quadruplicium dominicarum.
ã, ẽ, ĩ, õ, ũ, ãã, a-z, A-Z , Aa-Mm⁸ pp[196] 1-917
Inscribed 'Grantham Library' on t.p.
Repaired. Chain scars. 211x148
97.4 Tomus quartus concionum dominicarum aestivalium.
A-F⁸ G⁴ a-z, A-Z, Aa-Pp⁸ pp[104] 1-976
MS notes on end papers. Printer's waste of legal text in black letter in binding. 172x105
97.5 Tomus quintus concinionum quadruplicium super evangelia.
*-6*⁸ (-6* blank) a-z, A-Z, Ac-Ii⁸..... pp[96] 1-880 [+?]
Imperfect, wants all beyond Ii4.
MS notes on back free end paper. End papers from Latin legal text in black letter heavily annotated in all margins. (cf. 144, which has end paper from the same work)
Calf on board. 175x103
Not in Adams or BL

98 Summa praedicantium, ex omnibus locis communibus locupletissima.
Antuerpiae, ex officina Martini Nutij, 1600 4°
In two parts:
1. Tomus primus
*, A-Z, Aa-Mm⁸ pp[16] 1-559
2. Tomus secundus
**, AA-ZZ, Aaa-Lll⁸ (Lll 6-8 blank) pp[16] 1-538
Adams D454
Imperfect. Lll3/4 bound in after **3, leaves AA8 and BB1 removed by cutting, YY8 by tearing.
Note: Francis Trigge bequeathed 'Phillipus de dies his postell'.
Correspondence uncertain.
Calf on board. 213x155

DIONYSIUS CARTHUSIANI (Denys Van Leeuwen) (1402-1471)
99 In quatuor euangelistas enarrationes.
Coloniae, Petrus Quentell suis impensis excudebat, 1533 Fol.
A, B⁴ A-Z, a-g⁶ h⁸ i-z, aa-qq⁶ rr, ss⁴ ff[8] I-CCCLXXXIII
Adams D580
Four woodcut borders form compartment on title page.
Binding Old. 907 on oak, vellum MS binding slip. Chained. 334x216

DUNS SCOTUS (1266-1308)

100 Opera omnia [edition of Luca Waddingus Hibernus]
Lugduni, sumptibus Laurentii Durand, 1639 Fol.
Volume XI only of twelve, in two parts:
1. †, ††^{4} A-Z, Aa-Yy^{6} Zz^{4} Aaa^{6}(Aaa4, 5 blank)
Aaa6 is title leaf of Part II
2. a-z, aa-ll^{6} mm, nn^{4}
Title page signed : Guil. Ramsay
Calf on board, repaired, edges originally red. 365x236

101 Questiones super quattuor libris sententiarum.
(Venice, Bonetus Locatellus, 1497) Fol.
Parts iii and iv only in one volume.
iii Scotus super 3° sententarium.
a-g^{8} h, i^{6} (i6blank) 68 leaves, no numeration.
iv Scotus super 4°sententiarum.
aa-tt^{8} vv, xx^{6} (xx6 blank) 164 leaves, no numeration
BMC V,448 Hain 6420
Also bound in as part of volume is the separate work

102 Questiones quodlibetales Scoti.
AA-FF^{8} GG^{6} (-GG6, presumed blank) ff[1] 2-53
BMC V,449 Hain 6437
End papers (now free) are Latin MS on vellum, 2 cols with surrounding gloss. (14 century?)
Calf on oak, rebound with original leather,
Old.92, 93, 94 ('Heavy Binder')

103 Scriptũ primũ Oxoniense super primo sẽtẽtiarum.
[Venice, Gregorius de Gregorius, 1515] Fol.
Part 1 only out of 4:
a-v^{8} ff[1] 2-160
Adams D1124
Bound in with his Tabula generalis, 1516 (104)

104 Tabula generalis ac mare magnum Scotice subtilis octo sectiõibus vniversam ab A de Fantis.
(Venetijs, per Petrum de Quarengijs, 1516) Fol.
A^{8} D, E^{6} F^{4} G^{6}H^{4} A-O^{6} P^{4} 122 leaves not numerated
AdamsD1125
Also bound in : Scriptum primum Oxoniẽse, 1515 (103) and PETER LOMBARD: Sacratissima sententiarum, 1514 (266)
Francis Trigge bequeathed'Scotus his works' and the Catalogus librorum has 'Scotus libri ii'
Correspondence uncertain.
Signed: No. 12 Tho: Howett
Calf on oak, Old. 623 with 1014. Chained. 325x220

DURANTI, Guillelmus (c.1230-1296)

105 Rationale divinorum officiorum.
(Lugduni, [Jacques Maillet], 1499) (12 April) 4°
a-z, A-D^{8} E^{10} ff I-CCCIII
Black letter in two columns, first initial blank with guide letter, other initials 5-line woodcuts but many blank. Indice Generale degli Incunaboli delle Biblioteche d'Italia No.1947. No other copy of this edition recorded in British libraries. Front free end paper signed : William Irland with motto Soli deo honor & gloria.
Calf on board, repaired with original leather from binding by Richard Pynson. Front panel Old. (P) MISC.4, back AP5 with fleur de lys instead of bottom central dragon.250x165

EACHARD, Laurence (Archdeacon of Stowe) (c.1670-1730)

106 The History of England... 3 volumes:
London, for Jacob Tonson, 1708-18 Fol.
Volume II only
...from the beginning of the reign of Charles the First to the Restoration of Charles the Second... (1718)
c1, a^{2} b^{2} c2, V-Z, Aa-Zz,3A-5y^{4} 5z^{2} 6A-6G^{2} pp viii, 1-910 [26]

Red leather on board, gold tooled, title on spine, gilt edged, binding damaged by fitting of chain.
360x226

EDER, Georg (1523-1586)

107 [Oeconomia bibliorum, siue partitionum theologicarum libri quinque. Partitiones catechismi]
[Coloniae, apud Geruinum Calenium & haeredes Ioannis Quentelij 1582] Fol.
In two parts:
1. $^*a-^*f^4$ a-z, aa-zz, $3a-3n^6$ $3o^4$ pp[46] 1-714
Imperfect, wants a1
2. A^{*6} A^4 $B-K^6$ pp[10] 3-119
Adams E68
Calf on board, repaired.305x198

ENGLAND: STATUTES (Year books)
(7 Edw. III to 39 Edw. III, many years missing or out of order)
Nine years printed separately and bound together

108 47(sic) Edw. III. De termino Hillarii anno regni Edwardi tertii post conquestum septimo.
$A-L^6$ M^4 ff lxx
Colophon : Imprimis in edibus Richard Pynson 1518
Imperfect, wants A1. Worn Pynson device on M4 verso.
STC^2 9594

109 18 Edw. III. Hill, Decimo octauo Edwardi Tercii
$A-K^6$ ff liii
Printed at end : The prisce of thys book is xiid unbounde
STC^2 9558 [gives Wynkyn de Worde, 1516]

110 21Edw. III. De termino Hillarii anno regni regis Edwardi tertii vicesimo primo
$A-I^6$ ff liiii
Colophon : Londini in edibus Thome Bertheleti invico fletestrete prope aquagisi sitis sub intersignio Lucrecei excud. 1527
STC^2 9562

111 22-28 Edw. III. De termimo Hillarii anno regni... vicesimo secundo.
$A-R^6$ ff C (foliation upper case)
Colophon : Impress. Londini in edibus thome Bertheleti impressoris regii 1532 mense Nouembr
STC^2 9565

112 24 Edw. III. De termino Hillarii anno regni... vicesimoquarto.
$A-K^4$ (K4 blank) ff li
Colophon : Imprentyd by my(sic) Robert Redman [1528?]
STC^2 9569

113 29 Edw. III. Anno. xxix. E.tercii. De termino Hillarii...
$A-N^4$ ff lxiiii
Colophon : Imprinted at London by me Robert Redman [1535]
Pynson device (initials only) on N4 verso
STC^2 2570

114 30 Edw. III. Anno. xxx. E. tercii De termino Hillarii...
$A-G^6$ H^4 ff xlii
Colophon : Imprentyd at London by me Robert Redman [1535]
STC^2 9573

115 38 Edw. III.De termino Hillarii. Anno regni... tricesimo octauo.
$A-F^6$ G H^4 ff xliii
Colophon : Ex officina Pynsoniana cum privilegio a Rege inducto,Anno verbi incarnati 1520. Idibus martiis.
Pynson device on H4 verso
STC^2 9576

116 39 Edw. III. Anno xxxix. E. terci. De termino Hillari...
A-[$K^{6.4}$] ff [L]
Imperfect, has only K1-2 after I6
STC^2 9679 [gives R. Redman, 1534]
Items 108-116 bound together with original calf replaced on new oak.
Old. roll F.P. 282x199

117 Regis pie memorie Edwardi tertii a quadragesimo ad quinquegesimum, Anni omnes a mendis quibus miserrime scatebant repurgati et sui nitori restitute.
[40 Edw. III - 50 Edw.III]
Londini in aedibus Richardi Totteli 1555 Fol.
A^6 B-Z, Aa-Zz, 3A-3Z, A-T^4 V^6 (V6 blank)
Each year foliated separately
40 Edw. III ff[I] ii-xlix
Section followed by list of justices
41-45 Edw. III ff xxxi, xxvi, xlvi, xxviii, xxxiv
46-50 Edw. III ff xxxiv, xxvi, xxxiv, xxvii, xxvi
Colophon gives xiii January1556
STC^2 9582
No covers. 280x220

(1 Hen. VI - 20 Hen. VI, six years missing)
118 1 Hen. VI. (regis Henrici sexti i)
[A^6] B^4 (B4 blank) ff ix
Imperfect, wants A^6, begins ff vii
Colophon: Impressum Londini in aedibus Henrici Smyth, comoranti extra Temple Barre
STC^2 9619 [N. Hill, 1544?]

119 2 Hen. VI. (regis Henrici sexti ii)
[A^6] B^6...
Imperfect. Six leaves only, irregularly foliated ix, vii, x, x, xi, xii
Colophon as above
STC^2 9627 [N.Hill, 1544?]

120 3 Hen. VI. De termino Michaelis/Anno. iii. Henrici Sexti.
A-K^6 L^4 ff lvi
Colophon as above
STC^2 9633 [N. Hill, 1545?]

121 4 Hen. VI. De termino Michaelis/Anno regni Henrici sexti. iiii.
A-F^6 [F6 Blank] ff xxxi
Colophon as above
STC^2 9638 [N. Hill]

122 7 Hen. VI. De termino Michaelis/anno regni regis Henrici sexti/septimo
A-H^6 ff xlviii
Colophon as above
STC^2 9643 [N.Hill, 1545]

123 8 Hen. VI. De termino Michaelis/Anno regni regis Henrici Sexti, octauo
A-^{6} D-H^4 ff xxxviii
Colophon as above
STC^2 9649 [N. Hill, 1545?]

124 9 Hen. VI. De termino Pasche/Anno regni regis Henrici sexti/nono
A-K^6 L-M^4 (M4 blank) ff xlvii
Colophon as above
STC^2 9653 [N. Hill,1545?]

125 10 Hen. VI. De termino Michaelis. Anno. x. Henrici sexti.
A-D^6 E^4 (E4 blank) ff xxvii
Colophon as above
STC^2 9660 [N. Hill, 1545?]

126 11 Hen. VI. De termino Michaelis An. xi. H. vi.
$A\text{-}H^{6.4}$ I^4 K^2 $L\text{-}O^4$ ff lxix
Colophon as above
STC[2] 9965 [N. Hill, 1545?]

127 12 Hen. VI.De termino Michaelis. Anno. xii. Henrici sexti.
A^4 B^4 ff viii
Colophon : Imprynted at London by me Richard Tottle dwellinge in Fletestrete at the signe of the hand and the starre within Temple barre.
STC[2] 9670.5 [1553?]

128 14 Hen. VI. Anno. xiiii. Henrici Sexti.
A^6 B^4 C^6 D^8 ff xxvi
Colophon : Impressus per me Richardum Tottelum.
STC[2] 9677 [1553?]

129 18 Hen. VI. De Termino pasche. Anno. xviii. H. vj.
A^6 $B\text{-}H^4$ ff xxiiii
Colophon : Imprynted by Richard Tottel
STC[2] 9282.5 [1555?]

130 19 Hen. VI. De termino Michaelis. Anno. xix. H.vi.
$A\text{-}B^6$ $C\text{-}G^{4.6}$ H^6 I^4 $K\text{-}L^6$ M^4 N^8 $O\text{-}P^4$ Q^2 ff lxxx
Colophon : Imprinted at London in Fletestrete within Temple Barre at the signe of the hande and starre, by Richard Tottel
STC[2] 9688 [1555?]

131 20 Hen. VI. De termino Michaelis. Anno. xx. Henrici Sexti.
A^6 [B C] D^4 $E\text{-}I^{6.4}$... ff[?]
Imperfect wants B, C (10ff) and all beyond I4
STC[2] 9693 [1553?]
Volume containing items 118-131 has no covers. 282x226

132 Entry withdrawn.

1 Edw. V - 21 Hen. VI
Four items printed separately and bound together.
133 1 Edw.V. De termino Trinitatis anno. i. regni regis Edwardi quinti.
A, B^4 8 leaves not numerated.
Colophon : Imprinted at London in Fletestrete within Temple Barre, at the sign of the Hande and Starre, by Richard Tottel, the XII day of September in the year of oure Lorde 1555
STC 9897 is 1558

134 1 Rich. III. De termino Michaelis anno primo Richardii tertii.
A^4 ff iv
Colophon as above but not dated
STC 9906.7 [1556]

135 2 Rich. III.
A^8 B^4 C^6 D^4 ff xxii
Title page with woodcut having large initials WR in compartment 195x140 : incipit annus secundus Richard Tercjj. Impressum per me Henricum Smythe 1543
Not in STC[2]

136 1 Hen. VII - 21 Hen. VII (3 years missing)
London, in aedibus Richard Totteli, 1555
A^6 $B\text{-}D^4$ $2D^6$ E-Z, AA-ZZ, AAa-ZZz, $a\text{-}y^4$ x^6 $aa\text{-}mm^4$
Each year foliated separately.

1	Hen. VII	ff[2] [1] ii-xxvi
2-6	Hen. VII	ff xix, xv, xvii, xi, xvi
7-11	Hen. VII	ff xvi, xiii, xxvi, xxx, xxix,
12-16	Hen. VII	ff xxvii, xxviii, xxxii, xviii, xvii

then 20, 21 Hen. VII ff xiii-xli
Colophon exactly as 133
STC^2 9922
Marginal annotations throughout in Anglo-Norman. With woodcut title page of which top border shows the King in council and title Anni regis Henrici Septimi
Modern rebinding. 294x199

ERASTUS, Thomas (Thomas Liebler) (1524-1583)

137 Explicatio grauissimae quaestionis vtrum excommunicatio.
Pesclavii, apud Baocium Sultaceterum, 1589 4°
[actually London, J. Wolfe - name is anagram of editor Jacobus Castelvetrus]
A-Z, Aa-Cc^8 (-Cc8, presumed blank) pp[16] 1-390 [10]
STC^2 10511 Adams E912
Bound in with LAVATER : Liber primus Ezrae, 1586 (214)

EUSEBIUS PAMPHILI, Bishop of Caesarea (c.260-c.340)

138 The auncient ecclesiasticall histories of the first six hundred yeares after Christ... translated out of the Greek tongue by Meredith Hanmer, Doctor of Divinity...
London, printed by Richard Field, 1619 Fol.
¶ , A-Z, Aa-Zz, Aaa-Ddd^6 Eee^4 pp[12] 1-598 [18]
STC^2 10575
Calf on board, repaired. 294x186

139 Opera omnia (Ed. J. J. Grynaeus)
(Basileae, Sebastian Henricpetri, 1570) Fol.
Two volumes bound together:
I Includes : Evangelica preparatio, Evangelica demonstratio, Historia ecclesiastica.
a,α-δ^6 ε^4 A-Qq^8 Rr,Ss^6 Tt^4 Vv-Zz, AA-QQ^8 pp[60] 1-971
Wants a1
II Chronicon [trans. St. Jerome]
π1, A^6 π2,B-Z, Aa-Dd^6 Ee^2 Ff^4 ff[1] 6 [1] 7-160
π1, π2 are half-titles
A later edition of NE0195416
Binding Old. 775 on oak, repaired with board on back. Chained.328x205

FERUS, Johannes (Johann Wild) (1495-1554)

140 Annotationes in Exodum, Numeros, Deuteronomium, Lib. Iosuae, Lib. Iudicum...
Coloniae Agrippinae, apud haeredes Arnoldi Birckmanni, 1574 8°
*-$3*^8$ (3*8 blank) B-Z,Aa-Zz, 3A-$3Q^8$ ff[24] 1-488
Adams F348
Repaired. 176x106

141 [Enarrationes Actorum Apostolicorum]
[Coloniae, apud haeredes Arnoldi Birckmanni, 1567] Fol.
$[?]^4$ A-Y^6 (Y6 blank) pp[8?] 1-261
Imperfect, wants all before A
Copy in Trinity College, Dublin.
Calf on oak, repaired but since crazed by sun. Chain scars. 324x201
Note: Francis Trigge also bequeathed 'Ferus his Postill', possibly Postillae sive conciones in epistolas et evangelia not now extant.

142 Epitome sermonum : Huic adjectae sunt in Threnos Hieremiae prophetae conciones.
Coloniae, apud haeredes Arnoldi Birkmann, 1561 Fol.
In three parts:
1. $*^4$ A-O^6 P^8
^{6} p^{10} q-y^6 z^4 Aa^4 (Aa4 blank) ff 1-144
3. In threnos Ieremiae
A-F^6 G, H^4 ff 1-44
Adams F325
*4 is a woodcut of Crucifixion
Back end papers from waste sheet (sig z) with running title A Declaration of Spiritual Desertion.
(Not in Allison and Goldsmith : Titles of English Books 1475-1700)
Front end papers from printed statute, 3 leaves only (sigs B2, B3) of 13 Eliz. I, 3 : An Acte agaynste

Fugytyves over the sea, 1571
Signed : Johannes Rollinson pcru 5s.
Plain calf on board stamped I.R. (Iohannes Rollinson). Chain scar. 320x197

143 In Euangelium secundum Matthaeum commentaria, Romae recognita atque expurgata.
Romae, in aedibus Populi Romani,1577 8°
In two parts:
1. †, ††, A-Z, Aa-Rr^8 Ss^4 pp[76] 1-636
2. 3A-3Z, 4A-4Q^8 (4p8 blank) pp 1-606 [16]
Adams F371
Plain calf on board, repaired. 167x10

144 In sacrosanctum Iesu Christi Domini nostri Euangelium secundum Ioannem piae et eruditae iuxta Catholicam Doctrinam enarrationes...
Antuerpiae, apud viduam & haeredes Martini Nutij, 1565 8°
A-Z, Aa-Zz, 3A-3M^8 3N^4 3O-3Z^8 4A-4L8 (L8 blank) ff[5] 1-622 [7]
Adams F377
Signed on back end paper : Richard.....
Back end paper legal reports in contracted Latin, black letter with heavy marginalia.
(cf. 97.5, which has end paper from same work)
Inscription on title page : Autu Aegiph liber iste
Repaired. 175x105

145 Iobi Historia explicatio in CXIIII conciones eleganter distributa.....
Coloniae Agrippae, apud haeredes Arnoldi Birckmanni, 1574 8°
* (*8 blank), A-Z, Aa-Xx^8 ff[8] 1-354
Adams F350
End papers from rubricated manuscript on paper.
Repaired. Chain scars. 169x100

FESSEL, Daniel (1599-1676)
146 Adversorium sacrorum libri V.
Wittebergae, typis Iobi Wilhelmi Fincelli, 1650 4°
*, **,)(,):():(, 3):(, 4):(, a-o^4 A-Z, Aa-Zz, Aaa-Qqq^4 pp[160] 1-495 [1]
NF 0108605. Not in Adams.
Brown calf on board. Chained. 197x155

FITZHERBERT, Sir Anthony (1470-1538)
147 [La Graunde Abridgment collect par le judge tresreverend monsieur Antony Fitzherbert]
[London] (Richard Tottell 1565) Fol.
In two parts:
1. [?] F-Z, Aa-Yy^8 Zz^4 ff to 379
Imperfect, wants all to E and G1/2, begins f20
2. La secounde part (with title page) (in two sections)
iA, Bbb-Qqq^{8}Rrr$^{2-1}$ ff[1] 1-128
iiA^6 B-V, W^8... ff 1-166...
Imperfect, wants all after W
STC^2 10956
On front paste down Fitzherbert 1577 Fol. 35
Bad condition, front cover loose. 425x285

FITZHERBERT, Sir Anthony, and RASTELL, John
148 [La table coteynant en sommarie les choses notables en la graunde Abridgment] [compiled by Rastell]
(London, Richard Tottell, 1565) Fol.
[π]^1 a-z^8 Aa-Cc^8 Dd^4 (Dd4 blank) ff[1] 1-210
Imperfect, wants title page
STC^2 10956.5. See also COWLEY, John : Bibliography of Abridgments (1932) No. 56
Calf on board. Chain scars. 305x208

FOXE, John (1516-1581)

149 Eicasmi seu meditationes in sacram Apocalypsin.
[Londoni, [T. Dawson] impensis G. Byshop, 1587] Fol.
¶ , A-Z, Aa-Mm^6 Nn^4 (Nn^4 blank) pp[12] 1-396 [36]
Imperfect, wants ¶ 6
STC^2 11237
Bequeathed by Francis Trigge 1606
Repaired. Chained. 298x198

150 [History of the Acts and Monuments of the Church] (First volume only).
[London, Peter Short, 1596?] Fol.
A-B^6 AA-VV^6 Aaa-Vvv^6... pp[?] 3-714
Very imperfect, wants A1, all after Vvv and many pages loose or torn. Some illustrations cut out.
Probably STC^2 11226 to which pages correspond, but identification uncertain.
Signed : Peter Lely Jan 1709 on p.555
Doeskin on board, poor condition. 402x276

GALEN, Claudius(c.130-201)

151 Liber de plenitudine [to which are added three tracts]:
1. Polybus:
De salubri victus ratione privatorum Guintero Ioanne Andernaco interprete.
2. Apuleius Platonicus:
De herbarum virtutibus.
3. Benevenius, Antonius:
De Abditis nonnullis ac mirandis morborum & sanationum causis.
[Paris], apud Christianu VVechel, 1528 Fol.
In two parts:
1. aa-gg^6 ff 1-42
2. AA-CC^6 DD^4 ff 1-21
Adams G98
Back end paper has MS medical notes in Latin
Bound in with CELSUS : De re medicâ, 1528 (77)

GERSONUS, Iohannes (1363 - 1429)
Opuscula varia.
Included in ALLIACO : Imago mundi, 1483 (4)

GESNER, Conrad (1516-1565)

152 [Historiae animalium lib I - lib V (Ed. Jacobus Carronus)]
[Tiguri, in officina Froschouiana, 1587] Fol.
Books I, III, IV, V incomplete and bound as two volumes:

152.1 Lib. I De quadripedibus uiuiparis
a-z, A-Z, Aa-Yy^6.... pp 1092.....
Imperfect, wants a1, z, all beyond Yy

152.2 Very imperfect. Contains title page, dedication and index of Book V, and sections of Books III and IV rebound together but not in order, with many leaves missing.
NG 0178767
Calf on boards. Vol. II probably assembled from broken pieces in 1894. 359x219

GLASS, Salomon (1593-1656) (GLASIUS)

153 Philologiae sacrae qua totius sacrosanctae veteris et novi testamenti scripturae, tum stylus & literatura tum cencus & genuinae interpretionis ratio expenditur libri quinque. Editio secunda priori auctior.
Jenae, Sumptibus Zachariae Hertelii bibliopolae Hamburgensis litteris Steinmannianis, 1651 4°
Five books bound in three volumes:

153.1 Libri I, II
a-b, A-Z, Aa-Zz, Aaa-Zzz, Aaaa^4 pp[16] 1-532 [32]
NG 0248616 is this part only, dated 1643

153.2 Libri III, IV, dated 1645
a-b, A-Z, Aa-Zz, 3A-3Z, 4-4X, 5A-5Y^4 5Z^2 6A-6M^4 pp[16] 1-916 [96]
BL has this part only (12904 bb.10)

153.3 Liber V (Adds to imprint: imprimebat Christianus Laurentus Kempffius, 1651)
a-d (a1 blank), A-Z, Aa-Zz, 3A-3Z, 4A-4Z^4 pp[30] 1-598 [66]
Modern rebinding. 201x157

GODWIN (GODWYN), Thomas (d.1642)

154 Moses and Aaron. Civil and ecclesiastical rites used by the ancient Hebrewes... 7th Edition.
London, printed by S.G. for Andrew Crook and John Williams, 1655 4°
A^4 (A1 blank) B-Z, $Aa\text{-}Nn^4$ pp[6] 1-270 [8]
$Wing^2$ G977
On final blank half page is William Belby, Granthamiensi Lincolniasensi Librorium (sic), October 11, 1753.
Signed on front end paper : E. Holland
Calf on board. 190x142
Also bound in : Romanae historiae anthologia... 1658 (155) and ROUS : Archeologiae attica libri septem, 1658 (284)

155 Romanae historiae anthologia recognita et aucta. [and] English exposition of the Roman antiquities... For the use of Abingdon School.
London, for Henry Cripps of Oxford, 1658 4°
a, A-z, $Aa\text{-}Oo^4$ Pp^2 pp[4] 1-277 [23]
$Wing^2$ 988
Bound in with his Moses and Aaron, 1655 (154)

GRANTHAM, Thomas (Baptist) (1634 - 1692)

156 The Seventh-Day-Sabbath.
London, printed for the Authour, 1667 4°
$A\text{-}C^4$ pp[6] 1-18
$Wing^2$ G1547
Bound with : An answer out of the West, 1667 (11)

GRATIANUS (Bononiensis) (early 12th century)

157 Decretũ Aureum [with Margarita Decreti]
(Paris, Udalricus Gehring and Bertholdus Rembold, 1505) Fol.
In two parts:
1. a-z, A-Z, $aa\text{-}ff^8$ gg^{10} $hh\text{-}ll^8$ mm^4 (mm4 blank) $nn\text{-}oo^8$ p^{10} ff I-CCCCLIX [26]
Colophon on mm3
2. $AA\text{-}FF^8$ (-FF8 blank) ff I-XLV
AA1 begins: Margarita decreti seu tabula
Martiniana edita p fratrẽ Martinũ......
Adams G1038
Half bound calf on oak, front, vellum on board back, repaired. 410x286
The word 'papa' after the names of popes has been deleted untidily in thin ink throughout.

GREGORY (the Great) (Pope, c.540-604)

158 Omnia quae extant opera.
Paris, device of the Great Ship , 1586 (See 83) Fol.
Two volumes bound as one:
1. Tomus primus
††, ẽẽ, ĩĩ, $õõ^8$ ũũ, a-z, A-Z, $Aa\text{-}Nn^6$ pp[5] [VIII] IX-XXXVII, cols. 1-1414
2. Tomus secundus
A-Z, Aa-Zz, $3A\text{-}3Z^6$ $A\text{-}F^8$ G^{10} ff[1] cols. 5-1656
Wants G10
Adams G1175
Binding Old. 449 on oak (R.B.), repaired. Chained. 416x262

GREGORY IX (Pope, 1227-1241)

159 [Decretalium Gregorii libri V, (with commentary by Bernardus Bononiensis)]
(Paris, Berthold Rembolt, 1514) Fol.
Four parts with continuous signatures:
$[a^{10}]$ b-z, A-Z, $AA\text{-}KK^8$ LL^6
Imperfect, wants all before b, registrum gives a^{10}
The parts are:
i. Decretaliũ Gregorii ff I-CCCCXXII
ii. Tabula Bolognini (1472) 3 leaves not foliated
iii. Margarita Decretalium ff I-XVII
iv. Vita Gregorii noni 2 leaves

[by Raymundus Barchinonensis]
This edition not in Adams or BL as such, although Adams G1212 has same collation.
This copy, on HH7, has [Paris] ...opera et impẽsis Mgri Bertholdi Rembolt...1514 die vero xiiij Ianuarij
Half bound in calf with white vellum on board. 410x286

GREGORIUS NAZIANZENI (Saint, Patriarch of Constantinople) (329-389)

160 Orationes triginta octo [trans. Bilibaldo Pirckheymhero]. Tractatus, sermones libri aliquot.
Parisiis, in officina Claudii Chevalonii, 1532 Fol.
†, ††, †††, a-x^8 , y^6 (-y6 blank) ff[20] 1-173
Adams G1159
Calf on board. Side view roll of animals with roll of heads and initials RV in love-knot.
Not in Oldham. 348x231

[GRYNAEUS, Simon] (1493-1541)

161 Nouus Orbis regionum ac insularum veteribus incognitarum una cum tabula cosmographica.....
Basileae apud Io: Hervagium, 1555 Fol.
α, β, γ^8 (γ 8 blank) *, a-z, A-Z, Aa^6 Bb^8 pp[52] 1-677
Imperfect, wants gatherings p-t and map
Adams G1338
No covers. 325x197

GUALTHERUS (WALTHER, Rudolf, the Elder), (1519-1586)

162 In Acta Apostolorum per divum Lucam descripta homiliae CLXXV.
Tiguri, excudebat Christophorus Froschouerus, 1569 Fol.
aaa, a, b^6 c^4 a-z, A-Z, Aa^6 Bb^4 Cc^6 (Cc6 blank) ff[22] 1-291 [1]
Adams G1388
Half calf on oak board, rebound. Chained. 328x199

163 In D.Pauli apostoli epistolam ad Galatas homiliae LXI.
Tiguri, excudebat Christophorus Froschouerus, 1581 Fol.
a^6 b^8 (b8 blank) A-Z, Aa-Dd^6 ff[14] 1-162
Adams G1399
Bound in with his In epistolam ad Romanos homiliae, 1580 (164)

164 In D. Pauli apostoli epistolam ad Romanos homiliae.
Tiguri, excudebat Christophorus Froschouerus, 1580 Fol.
α, β^6 γ^8 a-z, A-P^6 Q^8 (Q8 blank) ff[20] 1-235
Adams G1394
Calf on board, repaired. Chained. 317x208
Also bound in : In epistolam ad Galatas homiliae LXI,1581 (163)

165 In evangelicum secundum Lucam homiliae CCXV.
(Tiguri, excudebat Christophorus Froschouerus, 1570) Fol.
$\alpha^6\beta^8$ (β8 blank) a-z, A-Z, Aa-Zz, 3A-3Z,AAa-CCc^6 (CCc6 blank) ff[1] 1-567
Imperfect. Wants α1 and fifteen other leaves
Adams G1376
Old. 771, but rebound. New chain attachment. 323x210

166 In Isaiam prophetam homiliae CCCXXVIII.
Tiguri, excudebat Christphorus Froschouerus, 1583 Fol.
**, α, β (β6 blank), a-z, A-z, Aa-Zz, AA^6 BB^4 CC^6 (CC6 blank) ff[17] 1-428
Adams G1361
Calf on board, repaired. Chain scars. 330x209

167 In prophetas duodecim quos vocant minores homiliae.
Tiguri, excudebat Christophorus Froschouerus, 1582 Fol.
3a-$3c^6$ $3d^8$ a-z, A-Z, Aa-Oo^6 Pp^8 ff[21] 1-353 [15]
Adams G1366
Calf on board, repaired. Chained. 319x205

HACKET, John (Bishop of Lichfield and Coventry) (1592-1670)

168 [A century of sermons upon several remarkable subjects... published by T. Plume]
[London, by Andrew Clark for Robert Scott, 1675] Fol.
A^2 $a\text{-}g^4$ h^2 B-Z, $Aa\text{-}Nnnnnn^4$ $Oooooo^{2\text{-}1}$ (+1) pp[1] 1-1013+errata sheet
Imperfect, wants A1
$Wing^2$ H169
Doeskin cover over older cover with gold tooling. 374x238

[HAWORTH, William (17thCentury)]

169 The Quakers Creed concerning the Man Christ.....
(London, printed for Jonathan Robinson) [1679] 4°
No signatures pp 1-16
$Wing^2$ H1197
Bound with : An answer out of the West, 1667 (11)

HEGESIPPUS (died c.180)

170 De rebus a Iudaeorũ principibus in obsidione fortiter gestis [Tr St.Ambrose]
Excudebat Iasper Gennepaeus apud sanctam coloniam, 1544 Fol.
A, $a\text{-}l^6$ m^8 (m4-m8 blank) ff[6] I-LXVII
Adams H149. Collation differs
Title page is woodcut with compartment. 116x75
Inscribed : 1590 4° Novembris
Bound in with VIGUERUS : Ad naturalem, 1555 (328)

HEMMINGIUS, Nicolaus (Hemmingsen, Niels) (1513-1600)

171 Commentaria in omnes epistolas apostolorum.
Impressum Argentorati, apud Theodosium Richelium, 1586 Fol.
a^8 A-Z, Aa-Zz, 3A-3Z, $4A\text{-}4V^6$ (Vuuu6 blank) pp[16] 1-981 [80]
Adams B1866
Rebound. 334x199

172 Commentariorum in Sacrosanctum Domine nostri Iesu Christi evangelium secundem Iohannem.
Basileae, per Conradum Waldkirch, 1590 Fol.
In two parts:
1.):(, a-z, $A\text{-}E^6$ F^4 G^6 ff[12] 2-651 [26]
2. $Aa\text{-}Vu^6$ pp1 - 433[25]
Adams H216
Title in compartment 160x100, within woodcut showing scenes from O.T.
Rebound calf on board. 330x204

173 Opuscula theologica in unum volumen collecta...
[Geneva], excudebat Eustathius Vignon, 1586 Fol.
(6 blank) a-z, A-Z, Aa-Zz, Aaa, Bbb^6 $Ccc\text{-}Eee^4$ ff[11] cols. 1-1680 ff[18]
Adams H209
Rebound. 352x223

HEYLYN, Peter (1599 - 1662)

174 Cosmographie in Four Books, containing all the Chorography of Historie of the Whole World, and all the Principall Kindoms, Provinces and Isles thereof... The second Edition.
London, Printed for Henry Seile, 1656-62 Fol.
$A\text{-}5H^6$ $5I^4$ pp[12] 1-1098 [20]
$Wing^2$ H1690
Bought of Rawson Hart Esq. by William Petty.
By him given to the Library of Grantham, 1742.
Signed : Rawson Hart.
Calf on board. 344x230

HIERONYMUS de Oleaster

175 Commentaria in Pentateuchum Mosi, hoc est in quinque primos bibliorum libri.
Lugduni, apud Petrum Landry, 1588 Fol.
$*^6$ $**^4$ a-z, A-Z, ss, $Bb\text{-}Gg^6$ Hh^8 $Ii\text{-}Ll^6$ Mm^4 (Mm4 blank) pp[20] 1-650 [56]
Adams O151
Back end papers are leaves ff74, 75 from the index to In Avicennae Libros (fol.)

Calf on board. Chain removed. 354x224

HILARY, Saint (of Poitiers) (c.315-c.367)
176 Lucubrationes quotquot extant [edited by Erasmus]
Basileae, per Eusebium Episcopium et Nicolai fratris haeredes, 1570 Fol.
α^6 β^8 a-z, Aa-Kk^6 Ll^8 Mm-Nn^6 Oo^8 pp[28] 1-684 [40]
Adams H556
Calf on board, repaired. Chain scars. 321x203

HOMILIES
177 [Certain sermons or homilies appointed to be read in churches.....]
[London, printed by Iohn Norton for Ioyce Norton and R. Whitaker, 1635] Fol.
Two volumes bound together:
I [?] A-H^6 I^2 (I2 blank) pp[?] -98
Wants preliminaries.
II Aa-Vv^6 $Yy^2$$Aaa^6$ Ddd^2 pp[4] 1-?
Very imperfect, pages and gatherings missing.
Probably STC^2 13661
No covers. Probably used in Grantham Church. 270x191

178 Certain sermons or homilies appointed to be read in......the time of Queen Elizabeth of famous memory : and thought fit to be reprinted.
London, Printed by T.R. for Andrew Crooke (et al), 1673 Fol.
A^{4-1} B-Z, Aa-Zz, Aaa-Ddd^4 pp[6] 1-388
$Wing^2$ C4091K
Reprints 1562 preface.
Probably used in Grantham Church.

HOSPINIANUS, Rudolphus (1542-1626)
179 De origine et progressu monachatus ac ordinum monasticorum equitumque militarium omnium libri VI.
Tiguri, in officina Froschouiana, 1588 Fol.
$*^6$ $**^4$ aa^6 bb^8 (bb8 blank) A-Z, a-z, Aa-Cc^6 Dd^4 Ee^6 (Ee6 blank) ff[23] 1-303
Adams H1038
End paper is cut from a broadsheet of Latin verses on the death of Robert Dudley, by Roger Williams 1588 (see 339)
Calf on board, repaired. 321x209

HRABANUS MAGNENTIUS (MAURUS, Rabanus) (776-856)
180 [Commentaria, antehac nunquam typis excusa, in Genesim libri IIII. Exodum libriIIII.]
[Cologne, I.Prael, 1532] 8°
a-z, aa-zz, aaa^8-? pp[?] 1-764 + [?]
Imperfect, wants preliminaries and all after bbb7.
NBi 0018340 is in four volumes and includes Numeros libri IIII and Deuteronomium libri IIII.
Rebound. 169x102

HUGHES, William (of Gray's Inn)
181 The Parsons lavv. Collected out of the whole body of the Common Law and some late reports.
London, printed for the Author,1641 8°
One volume in two parts:
1. π^1A^4 B-G^8 H^6 pp 1-108
2. Aa-Ii^8 pp 1-141
Back end paper from MS account book with items 'linnen and holland' to Elizabeth Barford dated 1626.
$Wing^2$ H3326
Brown leather. Poor condition, many pages loose. 149x94

[HUMFREY, John] (1621-1719)
182 A case of conscience, whether a nonconformist, who hath not taken the Oxford Oath, may come to live at London.
London, printed in the year 1669 4°
A-D^4 pp[2] 3-31
$Wing^2$ H3673

Bound with : An answer out of the West, 1667 (11)

183 The Healing Paper : or a Catholick Receipt for Union.
London, printed for B.T. and T.M., 1678 4°
$A^{2}B$-F^{4} pp[4] 3-31
$Wing^{2}$ H3680
Bound with : An answer out of the West, 1667 (11)

HUTCHINSON, John (Parish Clerk, d.1773)
184 A select set of psalms and hymns, with a choice collection of words, with proper tunes and basses, as they are appointed to be sung in the parish church of Grantham...Third edition
Grantham, W. Allen, 1792 oblong 4° pp[4] 96
Words engraved below music as far as p 82; then set in type.
Signed : William King
Caroline King 1802
Marbled boards, broken. 114x283

185 A selection of psalms and hymns intended to be sung in the Parish Church of Grantham. A new edition with considerable additions. (Words only)
Grantham, R. Storr, 1812 4°
pp 75
Signed : Thomas Hardy 1819, Mary Hardy
Presented by W.G. Holmes, 1923

186 A later edition, 1824 4°
pp 104

IRENAEUS, Saint, Bishop of Lyons(c.130-c.200)
187 Opus in quinque libros digestum.
Apud inclytam Basileam [Io.Froben], 1526 Fol.
a-z, A-E^{6} F^{8} g^{6} pp[12] 1-338 [12]
Adams I150
Woodcut borders on p1
Bound in with CLEMENT : Opera, 1526 (86)

JANSEN, Cornelius (1510-1576)
188 Commentarium in suam Concordiam, ac totam historiam Evangelicam, partes IIII.
Lugduni, apud Petrum Landri, 1591 Fol.
†, ††, A-S^{6} [T^{4}] V-Z, AA-QQ^{6} RR^{8} SS-ZZ, Aa-Nn^{6} Oo^{8} Pp-Zz, 3A-$3Z^{6}$ $4A^{4}$ (4A4 blank) pp[24] 1-1093 [20]
Imperfect, wants T^{4}
Adams J89 is 1590
Calf on board. 366x236

JEROME, Saint (c.342-420)
189 Opera omnia quae repereri potuerunt, diligentia & labore Mariani Victorii emendata... Quibus adjecimus Theophili Alexandrini epistolas tres...
Parisiis, apud Sebastianum Niuellium... excud. Henricus Thiery, 1578-79 Fol.
Nine volumes bound as three, with index:
189.1 Tomus I
ã, $ẽ^{6}$ a-n^{8} (n8 blank) ff[12] cols. 1-404
Fragment only of title page ã1
Tomus II
a-r^{8} s^{6} t^{2} ff[1] cols. 5-584
Tomus III
a-s^{8} t^{6} ff[1] cols. 5-498 [ff26]
Colophon gives Henricus Thiery 1578 on t6 recto.
Registrum add v^{4} but t6 verso is blank.
Tomus IV
a-z, A-Q^{8} R^{6} S^{6} ff[4] cols. 3-1276
Colophon as Tomus III, dated 1579
Binding Old.449 on oak, front board is from back of another book. 396x260
Imprint dated1579

189.2 Tomus V
a-y^8 z^6 (z6 blank) ff[1] cols. 5-682
Tomus VI
† ^{6} A-R^8 (r8 blank) ff[5] cols. 1-540
Tomus VII
A-Q^8 ff[1] 5-512
Front cover Old. 449 on oak, back board modern. Chained. 396x260
189.3 Tomus VIII
A-V^8 X^4 (X4 blank) ff[1] 9-652
Tomus IX
A^4 B-Z^8 Aa^6 (Aa6 blank) ff[2] cols. 1-732
Index....quam maxima diligentia collectus.
A-L^6 M^4 70 leaves of 3 columns, no numeration.
Registrum for all volumes.
Binding Old. 449 on oak. 396x260
All volumes as NH 0356995 but NUC date is 1602. Not in Adams.

JOHN DAMASCENUS, Saint (c.675-744)
190 (De orthodoxa fide liber)
(Parisiis, per Henricum Stephanum,1512) Fol.
A-Z^8 A-B^8 C^4 ff 1-203
Imperfect, wants a1
Not in Adams
Inscription on last page: frī Richardo crom[er] attinet iste liber ordinis sancti augustini conventus hulle.
The house at Hull is not mentioned in Ker: Medieval libraries of Great Britain (1964) and no other book with this provenance is recorded.
End papers are four leaves in conjugate pairs ff LXIX/LXXIII and ff LXVIIII/LXXV from Cornelius Roelans (1450-1523) De aegritudinibus infantium, Louvain, Jan Veldener, 1486.
Black letter, no signatures or catchwords, 29 lines, 'Greyhound' watermark. No other copies of these leaves are recorded as extant. See : D. E. Rhodes, 'A volume from the monastery library of Hayles'. Trans. Cambridge Bibliographical Soc. VIII, 1985,pp 598-603
Calf on oak. Old. 1003 (78) with 928

[JOHNSON, Robert]
191 The Gospell and his Maintenance.
London, printed by T. Cotes for Michael Sparke, 1633 4°
A-C^4 pp[8] 1-15 [1]
STC^{2}14692
Bound with : An answer out of the West, 1667 (11)

JOSEPHUS, Flavius (c.37-c.100)
192 Opera in sermonem latinum conuersa [trans. from Greek, Sigismund Gelen]
Basileae, ex officina Frobeniana, 1567 Fol.
†^{6} *^{4} a-z, A-Z, Aa-Zz, AA-Il^6 (Gg6 blank) pp[20] 1-910 [20]
Adams J366
Binding Old. 880 on oak boards, with remains of end papers from printed volume in black letter. Parts of text of an MS with red and blue rubrication are set off onto the board and the end papers. 346x220

193 Works [containing]
On the Antiquities of the Jews [and] The History of the Wars of the Jews.
London, for T. Bassett, N. Ranew, R.Chiswell and others, 1693 Fol.
A-Z, Aa-Zz, Aaa-Zzz^6 Aaaa^4(-Aaaa1.2) 4B, 4C^6 4D-4H^4 pp[6] 1-543 [10] 557-854 [6]
Wing^2 J1080
Separate title page for History of the Wars of the Jews on Aaa4, letter from Philo to Caligula on Aaaa4
Signed : Isaac Whitsed 1740, stamped A. Whitsed 1790
Bookplate N C Bray
p. 543 signed : C. Hinman December 15th 1729
Calf on board covered with old parchment deeds of Isaac Whitsed. Legible is, '... eleven years from 1745 at £80 per annum.' 375x234

JUNIUS, Franciscus (François Du Jon, Senior, 1545-1602)

194 Defensio catholicae doctrinae de S. Trinitate personarum in vnitate essentiae Dei.....
Heidelberg, [Commelinus] 1590-1 4°
In 3 volumes bound together:
I ã^{4} *^{2} A-P^{4} Q^{2} (Q2 blank) pp[12] 1-121 [1]
II (dated 1591)
(:), A-V^{4} (V4 blank) pp[8] 1-158
III (dated 1591)
(·:·), a-z, aa-ff^{4} gg^{2} pp[8] 1-235
Adams J459
Calf on board. Chain scars. 211x153

195 Expositio prophetae Danielis.
[Lyon?], excudebat Gabriel Carterius, 1594 4°
*, A-Z, AA-PP^{4} QQ^{2} pp[8] 1-299 [9]
Not in Adams or BL but Univ. of Edinburgh catalogue gives [Geneva?]
Bound in with his Lectiones in Ionam prophetam, 1594 (196)

196 Lectiones in Ionam prophetam.
[Heidelberg], in officina Sanctandreana, 1594 4°
A-I^{4} (I4 blank) pp 1-86 [1]
Adams J478
Also bound in : Expositio prophetae Danielis, 1594 (195) and TERTULLIAN : De pallio liber, 1595 (311)
Calf on board. 205x137

197 Libri Geneseos analysis...
[Heidelberg], in officina Sanctandreana, 1594 4°
*^{4} (*4blank) A-Z, Aa-Dd^{4} pp[6] 1-214
page 214 is numbered 175
Not in Adams.
Bound in with his Vita Iunii, 1595 (199)

198 Libri II Mosis qui Exodus vulgo inscribitur, analytica explicatio.
Lugduni Batauorum, ex officina Plantiniana apud Franciscum Raphalengium, 1597 4°
*, **,***, A-X^{4} (X3, 4 blank) ff[12] 1-163
Adams J474. Collation differs.
Bound in with his Vita Iunii, 1595 (199)

199 Vita Francisci Iunii ... ab ipso nuper conscripta. [Ed. P. Merula]
Lugduni Batauorum, ex officina Plantiniana. Apud Franciscum Raphelengium, 1597 4°
*,**, A-I^{4} pp[16] 1-72
Adams J473
On title page Grantham Library
Calf on board. Chain scars. 205x145
Also bound in : Libri Geneseos analysis, 1594 (197) and Libri II Mosis analytica explicatio, 1597 (198)

JUSTIN, Saint and Martyr (c.100-c.165)

200 Τα ευρισκομενα - Opera
[Heidelberg] Ex typographeio Hieronymi Commelini, 1593 Fol.
)(. A-Z, Aa-Ii^{6} Kk^{8} Ll-Oo^{4} Pp^{6} Qq-Xx^{4} (Xx4 blank) pp I-XII, 1-490
Greek and Latin in parallel columns
Adams J498
Calf on board, repaired. 341x218

KINGE, John (Bishop) (1559-1621)

201 [Lectures upon Jonas...delivered at York in the yeare of our Lorde 1594]
(Oxford, J. Barnes, 1597) 4°
*^{6} A-Z, Aa-Xx^{8} Yy^{4} (Yg4 blank) pp[6] 1-706 Imperfect, wants *1, 2
Tt3 is a title page : A sermon preached at the funeralles.....
Printed at Oxford by Joseph Barnes, 1597.
STC^{2} 14976

Also bound in is BABINGTON : A very fruitful exposition of the Commandments, 1596 (26)
Calf on board. Chain scars. 208x151

LANFRANC de ORIANO (d.1488)

202 Repetitiones disputationes necnon tractatus diversorum doctorum.
(Venice, Vindelinus de Spira for Johannes de Colonia, 1472) Fol.
227 unnumbered leaves without signatures, the first blank.
BMC V,161
Half calf on oak board, modern repair by HMSO. 431x291
Also bound in is STEPHANUS de CAIETA : Repetitio, 1476 (305) and SONCINUS, Marianus : Repetitio sententiam sanguinis, 1476 (295)

LARGUS, Scribonius

De compositionibus medicamentorum.
See CELSUS : De re medicâ, 1528 (77) of which it forms part.

LATOMUS, Jacobus (the Elder) (1475-1544)

203 Sacra theologiae opera.
Louanii, excudebat Bartholemaeus Grauius, 1550 (July 29) Fol.
a, a-z, Aa-Mm^6 Nn^4 ff[6] 1-214
As Adams L263, but date not altered.
Modern rebinding, original calf on new oak, Old. 871 with 829
Front paste down was MS on vellum.
Only a fragment remains, but a set-off of the manuscript was left on the front cover board. A photocopy of this is now on the new board: the old one disintegrated. (note by M.A. Phipps, 1952).
320x201
Wrongly marked Peter Latom on fore-edge.

LAVATER, Ludovic (1527-1586)

204 In libros Paralipomenon siue Chronicorum commentarius.
Tiguri, excudebat Christophorus Froschouerus, 1573 Fol.
α^6 β^4 a-z, A-N^6 O^8 ff[10] 1-224
Adams L309
Calf on board, repaired 335x209.

205 In librum Iosue invictissimi imperatoris Israelitarum homiliae LXXIII.
Tiguri, apud Christophorum Froschouerum, 1576 Fol.
*, A-N^6 O^8 (O8blank) ff[6] 1-85
Adams L306
Also bound in : Liber Iudicum homiliis CVII, 1585 (209) and Liber Iobi homiliis CXLI, 1585 (208)
Calf on board, repaired. 319x206

206 In librum Proverbiorum sive sententiarum Solomonis
Tiguri, apud Christophorum Froschouerum, 1586 Fol.
α, β^6 g^8 a-z, Aa-Ee^6 Ff^4 Gg, † (†6 blank), Hh-Pp^6 Qq^4 ff[20] 1-228 [2]
Adams L318
Also bound in : Propheta Ezechiel homiliis, 1581 (212) and Liber Hestherae homiliis XLVII, 1585 (207)

207 Liber Hestherae homiliis XLVII expositus.
Tiguri, excudebat Christophorus Froschuerus, 1585 Fol.
a, b (b6 blank), A-O^6 P^4 Q^6 (Q6 blank) ff[12] 1-93
Adams L313
Bound in with his In librum proverbiorum, 1586 (206)

208 Liber Iobi homiliis CXLI. Germanica lingua explicatus.
Tiguri, excudebat Christophorus Froschouerus, 1585 Fol.
α^6 β^4 A-Z, a-r^6 s^4 t^6(t6 blank) b^6 (b6 blank) ff[10] 1-249 [5]
Adams L314. Collation differs.
Bound in with his In librum Iosue, 1576 (205)

209 Liber Iudicum homiliis CVII expositus.
Tiguri, excudebat Christophorus Froschouerus, 1584 Fol.
aa^6 bb^4 $A\text{-}X^6$ Y^4 Z^6 (Z6 blank) ff[10] 1-135
V-Z is an added section in italic:
De patientia christiana in perseqvvatione.
Adams L307
Bound in with his In librum Iosue, 1576 (205)

210 Liber Nehemiae qui est secundus Ezrae dicitur homiliis LVIII expositus.
Tigurinae, in officinis Froschouiana 1586 4°
α – ζ; a-z, $a\text{-}e^4$ (e4 blank) ff[24] 1-111
Adams L312
Bound in with his Liber primus Ezrae, 1586 (211)

211 Liber primus Ezrae homiliis XXXVIII expositus.
Tigurinae, in officinis Froschouiana, 1586 4°
$*^4$ (*4 blank) $A\text{-}Y^4$ (Y4 blank) ff [3] 1-81 [6]
Adams L311
Also bound in : Liber Nehemiae, 1586 (213) and also ERASTUS : Explicatio gravissimae quaestiones, 1589 (137)
Calf on board, repaired, Chain scars. 213x149

212 Propheta Ezechiel homiliis seu potius commentariis expositus. Editio secunda.
Genevae, apud Eustathium Vignon, 1581 Fol.
$¶^4$ a-z, $aa\text{-}mm^6$ nn^8 (nn8 blank) ff[4] 1-210 [6]
Adams L320, but wants diagram.
Bound in with his In librum proverbiorum, 1586 (206)

LEO MAGNUS, Pope (d.461)

213 Epistolae decretales ac familiares.
Antuerpiae, apud Philippum Nutium, 1583 8°
$a\text{-}v^8$ x^2 pp[2] 3-316 [7]
Adams L452
Bound in with his Opera, 1583 (214)

214 Opera.
Antuerpiae, apud Philippum Nutium, 1583 8°
A Z^8 $Aa\text{-}Bb^8$ Cc^4 ff[1] 2-193 [13]
Adams L449
Repaired. 170x110
Also bound in : Epistolae decretales ac familiares, 1583 (213)

LEONARDUS de UTINO

215 Sermones quadragesimales de legibus.
(Paris, Ulrich [Gering], Martin [Crantz] and Michael [Friburger] 1477]
Black letter, two columns of 60 lines, no catchwords or signatures ff 1-303
BMC VIII,9 (IC. 39081) Hain 16118
Rubricated in red and blue.
Rebound buckram with half calf. 406x289

LITURGY

216 The Book of Common Prayer.
(London, Robert Barker and assigns of John Bill, 1634) 4°
π, $A\text{-}E^8$ F^6 47 leaves not numerated
Imperfect. No title page
STC^2 16396
State prayer for 'Queene, Mary, Prince Charles and the rest of the royall progenie'.
Also bound in are SPEED : The genealogies recorded in the Sacred Scriptures, (298), STERNHOLD and HOPKINS : The whole book of Psalms, 1634 (303) and Bible (Barker and Bill, 1634) (49).
Signed : William Durham, Richard Durham of Sidebooke (?) in the Countty (sic) of Linkoune, 1650
Presented by John Cheshire, 1948. Modern Grantham binding, extensively repaired. 227x171

217 The Book of Common Prayer, with Psalter.
London, printed by His Ma[ties] Printers, cum privilegio, 1669 Fol.
a-z, aa-rr^6 ss^4 no page numeration
Wing^2 B3635
Black letter, red rules inserted by hand.
Inscribed as presented by Dr. Fuller, Bishop of Lincoln, 1671 and as 'having the Corporation of Grantham's Arms upon them.'
Signed : Sam. Burnett [Vicar 1670-1710]
Rebound (early 19th century ?) in red leather, without arms, gilt edged. 321x198
217a Another copy of this edition, bound and inscribed as above.

218 The Book of Common Prayer
London, Assigns of Thomas Newcomb and Henry Hills, 1711 12mo
π^2 A-O^{12} P^6 no pagination
Additional title page : The Liturgy of the Church of England adorned with 55 Historical Cuts (with frontispiece of Queen Anne). Sold by John Sturtin, Golden Lion Court in Aldersgate Street and John Nott in the Savoy.
Red rules inserted by hand.
Black leather on board, silver clasps and mountings, name plate engraved R.M. 1754
On end paper : Gift of Robert Mulligan to his grandson Robert Mulligan Charnley, Mint Street, Southwark.
Presented by Miss Lilian Scott, 1950 (see article in Parish Magazine, May 1950)
Also bound in STERNHOLD and HOPKINS : The whole book of Psalms, 1703 (305)

219 The Book of Common Prayer, with Psalms.
London, printed by John Baskett, and by the assigns of Thomas Newcome and Henry Hills, deceased 1715 4°
a-b^8 c^2 A^4 B-Y^8 *^{4} no pagination
Printers numbers 4, 6. Red rules inserted by hand.
Signed : John Knipe
Also bound in STERNHOLD and HOPKINS : The whole book of Psalms, 1708 (306)
19th century binding in red leather, gilt edges, in bad condition. 236x178

220 The Book of Common Prayer.
London, John Baskett, 1737, Price six-pence. 12mo
π^1 A-L^{12} no pagination
Many woodcuts inserted as plates blank on verso
Calf on board, broken at hinges.
Also bound in STERNHOLD and HOPKINS : The Psalms in Metre, 1737 (307)

LIVY (Titus Livius Patavini) (59 B.C.E - 17 C.E)
221 Historiam omnium Romanorum...(accessit) Chronologia in Titi Livii historiam, accommodata ad tabulas capitolinas Verrii Flacci.
Francofurti ad Moenum, apud Joannem Wechelem, 1588 Fol.
In three parts:
1. α^4 β-d$^{6\ 8}$ A-Z, AA-ZZ, 3A-3D^6 3E-3O^4 pp[6] 1-682
Wants α4(blank)
2. Chronologia
4A-4E^6 pp[2] 3-59
3. *^{4} (*4 verso blank) Aa-Zz, 3A-3Z, 4A-4C^6 4D^4 pp[7] 1-613
Adams L1350
Signed : Richard Symons 1616 Feb 7 pret 12^s
Coll. Magdal. Camb.
Binding Old, 771 on oak, rebound. 402x249

[LLOYD, William] (1627-1717)
222 A seasonable discourse shewing the necessity of maintaining the established religion in opposition to Popery. The fourth edition.
London, printed for Henry Brome, 1673 4°
A-E^4 pp[2] 1-37 [1]
Wing^2 L2696
Bound with : An answer out of the West, 1667 (11)

LUBBERTUS, Sibrandus (1556-1625)

223 De Papa Romano libri decem.
Apud Aegidium Radaeum ordinum Frisiae typograph in Academia Franekerana, 1594 8°
✠^{6} A-Z, Aa-Zz, aAa-nNn^{8} oOo^{2} pp[12] 1-903 [14]
Adams L1545
Calf on board, repaired. 165x103

224 De principiis Christianorum dogmatum libri septem Collati cum disputationibus Roberti Bellarmini.
Franekerae, apud Aegidium Radaeum ordinum Frisiae Typographum in Academia Franekerana, 1591 8°
*^{4} A-Z, Aa-Zz, Aaa-Bbb^{8}Ccc^{4} pp[8] 1-773 [3]
Adams L1546
Inscription on front end paper signed : G.L.
Calf on board. 160x102

LYCOSTHENES, Conrad (1518-1561)

225 Similium loci communes....editi cum T.Z.[Zwingerus] Bas. similitudinum methodo.
Basileae, ex officina Episcopiorum,1575 8°
α-η, a-z, A-Z, Aa-Ss^{8} pp[2] 3-1002 [1]
NL 0581464. Not in Adams.
Heavy marginalia. End of book signd : Thomas Richardson.
Calf on board. 198x125

MAGDEBURG CENTURIATORS [FLACIUS, Matthias (1520-1575) et al]

226 Ecclesiastica historia...secundum singula centurias...per aliquot studiosos et pios viros in urbe Magdeburgica [Adams M110 Edition B]
Basileae, per Ioannem Oporinum, 1560-74 Fol.
Thirteen centuries bound in 8 volumes:

226.1 (In four parts)(1560):
- i. Prima centuria liber primus
  α-γ^{6} a-t^{6} (t6 blank) ff[18] cols. 1-382 ff[18]
- ii. Prima centuria liber secundus
  αα^{4} A-Z, Aa-Ii^{6} Kk^{8} ff[4] cols. 1-684 ff[24]
- iii. Secunda centuria
  ††^{4} aa-cc^{4} dd-nn^{6} oo^{4} pp^{6} ff[4] cols. 1-283 ff[11]
- iv. Tertia centuria
  ^{4} (4 blank) aaa-mmm^{6} nnn^{8} ooo-qqq^{6} (qqq6 blank) ff[3] cols. 1-320 ff[17]

Adams M110.1a, M110.2a, M110.3a (no colophon on qqq6)

226.2 Quarta centuria (1560)
a-z, A-Z, Aa-Zz, AA-EE^{6} FF^{4} pp 11, cols. 13-1574 pp[57]
Adams M110.4

226.3 Quinta centuria (1562)
α, a-z, A-Z, Aa-Rr^{6} Ss^{4} Tt-Yy^{6} Zz^{4} (Zz4 blank) ff[6] cols. 1-1526 ff[27]
Adams M110.5. Colophon on Zz3 verso

226.4 (In two parts):
- i. Sexta centuria (1562)
  a-z, A-R^{6} S^{4} T^{6} (T6 blank) pp 14, cols. 15-872 pp[54]
- ii. Septima centuria (1567) pp 20, cols. 21-668 pp[51]
  a-z, A-D^{6} E^{8} F-H^{6} I^{8} (I8 blank)

Adams M110.6a (date in roman), M110.7

226.5 (In two parts):
- i. Octava centuria (1564)
  α, a-z, A-P^{6} Q^{8} R, S^{6} T^{8}. ff[6] cols. 1-640 ff[20]
- ii. Nona centuria
  a^{4} b, a-z, A-C^{6} D^{4} E, F^{8} (F8 blank) ff[10] cols. 1-640 ff[13]

Adams M110.8, M110.9

226.6 (In two parts):
- i. Decima centuria (1567 in arabic)
  a-z, A-F^{6} G^{8} H-I^{6} K^{8} (K8 blank) pp 6, cols. 7-723 pp[38]
- ii. Undecima centuria (1567)
  a-z, A-M^{6} N^{8} (N8 blank) pp 14, cols. 15-766 pp[44]

Adams M110.10, M110.11

226.7 Duodecim centuria (1569)
a-z, A-Z, Aa-Zz, AA-OO^6 PP^4 QQ^6 pp 8, cols. 9-1930 [47]
Adams M110.12

226.8 Decimatertia centuria (1574)
a-z, A-Z, Aa-Ll^6 Mm^4 Nn-Pp^6 Qq^8 (Qq8 blank) pp 9, cols. 9-1378 pp[49]
Adams M110.13
All volumes plain calf on board. I and IV are chained, all others have chains torn off. All 330x210

MARLORAT, Augustin (1506-1562)

227 Novi Testamenti catholica expositio. Editio IIII.
Geneuae, apud Petrum Sanctandreanum, 1585 Fol.
In two volumes:

227.1 Matthaeus - Acta Apostolorum.
*^{4} a-z, A-T^8 pp[8] 1-672

227.2 Romanos - Apocalypsin.
aaa-zzz^8 Aa-Vv^8 (Vv8 blank) ¶a-¶c^8 ¶d$^{6-1}$ pp 1-686 [60]
Adams M620
Both volumes calf on board with coat of arms and motto.......IA VNA (?). 404x235

MASIUS, Andreus (1514-1573)

228 Iosuae imperatoris historia.
Antuerpiae, ex officina Christophori Plantini, 1574 Fol.
In two parts:
1. Text (Hebrew, Latin translation, Septuagint, Latin translation, in four columns, with Vulgate across page at bottom)
A-N^6 (N6 blank) pp[2] 3-154
2. Commentariorum in Iosuam
a-z, Aa-Ee^6 Ff^8 Gg^6 Hh^8 pp 1-350 [30]

Adams B1325
Calf on board. 335x225

MEDE, Joseph (1586 - 1638)

229 The vvorks of the Reverend, judicious & learned Divine, Mr. Joseph Mede, B.D...formerly printed, but now revised & sundry discourses never before published
London, printed by M.F. for John Clark, 1648 4°
In two parts:
Part 1
a. Diatribae : Discourses on divers texts.
b. Diatribae : or a continuation of certain discourses.
c. The Christian sacrifice...foretold by the prophet Malachi.
A-P^8 Q^4 Aa^2 (Aa1 blank) Bb-Tt^8 pp[12] 1-527

Part 2
a. The name Altar...anciently given to the Holy Table
b. Churches...appropriate places for worship
Aaa-Ggg^8 Hhh^2 Ppp^6 pp[12] 1-78 [12]

Wing^2 M1585
The following tracts are also bound in:

230 The key of the Revelation...(Tr. from the Latin by Richard More).
Printed in London by R.B. [R. Bishop] for Phil. Stephens, 1643
In two parts:
i. A, a, b, B-Q^4 R^2 pp[20] 1-133
ii Aa-Ss^4 pp 1-135 [9]

Wing^2 M1595

231 The reverence of Gods house (1638)
A-K^4 (A1 blank) pp[2] 1-71
Not in Wing^2

232 Daniel's VVeekes.
[London, M.F. for John Clark, 1643]
$A\text{-}G^4$ pp[2] 1-53
$Wing^2$ M1595

233 A paraphrase and exposition of the profesie of St. Peter.
London, printed by R. Bishop for Samuel Man, 1642
$A\text{-}D^4$ pp[2] 1-25
$Wing^2$ M1605

234 The apostasy of latter times.
London, printed by L.N. for Samuel Man.... 1644
A, a, $B\text{-}V^4$ pp[16] 1-152
$Wing^2$ M1590
On end paper : This book belongs to the Grantham Library and was sent to me by th^e Rev^d. Mr. Mills to be lodged here. March 1717
Jo. Harrison
[Vicar 1710-36]
Calf on board, repaired. 199x144

MEENE, Joshua (Vicar of Wymondham)
235 A liberall maintenance is manifestly due to the Ministers of the Gospell.
London, printed by Thomas Harper for Laurence Chapman and William Certain, 1638 4°
$A\text{-}K^4$ L^2 pp[8] 1-74
STC^2 17780
Typis mandetur Sam. Baker, Feb. 6 1637
Bound with : An answer out of the West, 1667 (11)

MERCERUS, Johannes (d.1570)
236 [Commentarij in librum Iob. Adjecta est T.Bezae epistola.]
[Geneuae, excudebat Vignon, 1573] Fol.
*, a-z, $A\text{-}H^6$ I^4 (I4 blank) $a\text{-}b^6$ ff[11] 1-189
Imperfect, wants *1
Adams M1314
Rebound in brown suede. 312x193
Also bound in : In Salomonis, Prouerbia, Ecclesiasten & Canticum Canticorum, 1573 (237)

237 Commentarij in Salomonis, Prouerbia, Ecclesiasten & Canticum Canticorum.
Geneuae, excudebat Eustathius Vignon, 1573 Fol.
$*^2$ a-z, $A\text{-}F^6$ (F6 blank) ff[2] 1-168 [4] [1]
Adams M1315
At end, a table of harmonies between the above books ff[4]
Bound in with his Commentarii in librum Iob, 1573 (236)

238 Commentarii locupletiss in prophetas quinque priores inter eos qui minores vocantur...
[Geneva, Henricus Stephanus, II, 1570] Fol.
π^4 (π4 blank) a-z, $A\text{-}P^6$ Q^4 pp[5] 1-464
Adams M1318
Binding Old. 449 on board (R.B.). Chain scars. 342x221

239 In Genesin commentarius
Geneuae, ex typographia Matthael Berjon, 1598 Fol.
¶^{2} a-z, A-Z, Aa-Pp6 Qq-Rr4 pp[4] 1-747
Imperfect, wants g1. M6, N1 are signed N, M2
Adams M1312 continues collation to Yy, but this copy appears to be complete at p.747.
Binding Old. 449 (R.B.) on board, repaired, water stained. Chain scars. 342x216

MILIS, Iohannes de

240 [Repertorium (in jure canonico)]
(Basel, Nicolaus Kesler) [1488] Fol.
π1, $a^6\pi$2, b^8 c^6 d-e^8 f^6 g^8 h-i^6 k^8 l-p^6 q^8 r^{6-1} t^6 v^8 x-y^6 z^8 115 leaves not numerated
Wants π1 (verso blank?), corner of z8 torn.
Black letter, two cols. of 56 lines, blank initials without directors.
BM III,766 (IB 37602) Hain* 11156
End papers from quarto work of rhetoric, black letter 35 lines per page (91 mm/20 lines) signature k, k2.
No covers. 300x220

MOLLER, Henricus (1530-1589)

241 Enarrationis Psalmorum Davidis...postremo editio... accesserunt theses seu observationes [et] D.Th.Bezae eorundem Psalmorum paraphrasis poetica.
Genevae, apud Guillelmum Laemariam, 1591 Fol.
¶, A-Z, Aa-Zz, 3A-$3Z^6$ α-γ^4 pp[12] cols. 1-1666 pp[24]
This edition not in Adams but collation agrees Adams M1579
Binding Old. 449 (R.B.) repaired. Chain scars. 368x223

242 Iesaias, in Iesaiam prophetam commentarius.
Tiguri in officina Froschouiana, 1588 Fol.
aa, bb^6 cc^8 A-Z, a-p^6 q^8 ff[20] 1-236
Adams M1578
Binding Old. 449 (R.B.). 317x192

MORE, Henry (1614-1687)

243 [A collection of several philosophical writings of H. More.]
[London, J. Flesher for Wm. Morden, Cambridge, 1662] Fol.
[?] [A-F?] G-Z, Aa-Zz, Aaa-Vvv^8
Imperfect, wants all before G and pp 91-152
Contains five works with separate title pages and pagination:

1. Antidote against atheism. pp[?] -190 [11]
2. A brief discourse of enthusiasm. pp 1-48 [3]
3. Henrici Mori epistolae quatuor ad Renatum Des-cartes. pp[1] 55-133 [pagination follows 243.2 above]
4. The immortality of the soul. pp[6] 1-234 [12]
5. A conjectural essayof interpreting the mind of Moses according to a threefold Cabbala. pp[6] 1-184 [16]

$Wing^2$ M2646
No covers. 301x190

244 Enchiridion ethicum praecipua moralis philosophiae rudimenta complectens....
Editio secunda : Cui accessit auctoris epistola ad V.C.
Londoni, excudebat. J. Flesher, venale autem habetur apud Guilielmam Morden bibliopilam Cantabrigiensem,1669 8°
Two parts, continuous signing
A, (a), B-R^8 pp[32] 1-227 [12] 1-54
R4 recto is title page of Epistola ad V.C.
$Wing^2$ M2653
Calf on board, repaired.
Slip cut from earlier end paper 'Ex dono auctoris'. 170x106

245 Enchiridion metaphysicum. Pars prima
Londoni, Typis E. Flesher prostat apud Guilielmum Morden bibliopilam Cantabrigiensem, 1671 4°
¶, A-Z, Aa-Zz, Aaa-Kkk^4 (Kkk3, 4 blank) pp[8] 1-403 [2]
$Wing^2$ M2654
Repaired cover has slip from former end paper 'Ex dono auctoris'
Repaired. 204x150

Epistola ad V.C....quae... Apologiam complectitur pro Cartesio, quaeque introductionis loco esse poterit ad universam philososphiam cartesianam.
See his Enchiridion Ethicum, 1669, (244) of which it forms part.

246 An explanation of the grand mystery of godliness...
London, printed by J. Flesher, for W. Morden, Bookseller in Cambridge, 1660 Fol.
A^8 a, B-Z, Aa-Zz, Aaa-Ggg^6 (Ggg6 blank) pp[28] 1-546 [77]
$Wing^2$ M2658
On front paste down 'Ex dono auctoris'
Calf on board. Chained. 307x196

247 A modest enquiry into the mystery of iniquity...
London, printed by J. Flesher for W. Morden, Bookseller in Cambridge, 1664 Fol.
A-Z, Aa-Zz, Aaa-Ccc^6 (Ccc6 blank) pp[12] 1-567 [4]
$Wing^2$ M2666
Two parts are printed and paged continuously but there is a separate title page on R2 recto
Calf on board. Chained. 297x192

248 Opera philosophica tum quae Latine tum quae Anglice primitus scripta sunt...
Londoni, J. Macock impensis J. Martyn & Gualt. Kettilby, 1679 Fol.
In 3 volumes:

248.1 Containing 11 works.
a, a(repeat)-c, A^4 (A2 blank) B-Z, Aa-Zz, 3A-3Z, 4A-4Z, 5A-$5N^4$ $5O^2$ pp XXIV [2] 1-722 [60]
Imperfect, wants (first) a4; (first) a1and a2 follow c4
Inscribed : Sep 20 1679 Ex dono reverendi auctoris
in the years of John Smyth church warden.
Contains diagrams and plates
Calf on board. 376x240

248.2 Containing 5 works.
A-Z, Aa-Zz, 3A-3Z, 4A-4Z, 5A-$5C^4$, 5D-$5L^2$ pp[2] 1-758 [32]
Inscribed as above
Calf on board, repaired. 372x238

248.3 Containing 11 works.
[π]A-D^2 E-Z, Aa-Zz, Aaa-Zzz, 3A-3Z, 4A-4Z, $6A^4$ 6B-$6L^2$ pp[18] 1-908[36]
Imperfect, wants π
Colophon dated 1674, illustrated
Calf on board, repaired, gold tooled flowers on spine. Chain scars. 372x235
All volumes $Wing^2$ M2634

249 A plain and continued exposition of the several prophecies...of the Prophet Daniel.
London, By M.F. for Walter Kettilby, 1681 4°
A, a-m, B-Z, Aa-Ss^4 (Ss3, 4 blank) pp CIII, 314 [2]
$Wing^2$ M2673
On front end paper : Mar 12 Anno Dom 16 $^{80}/_{81}$
Ex dono reverenti auctoris
Also inscribed : This book belongs to Grantham Library. Borrowed by me Samuel Burnitt [vicar 1670-1710]
Borrowed by me William Fell Aug 20th 1776
Repaired. 210x157
Also bound in : Tetractys anti-astrologica, 1681 (250)

250 Tetractys anti-astrologica...wherein the....weaknesses of John Butler B.D. his A vindication of Astrology...are laid open.
London, M.F. for Walter Kettilby, 1681 4°
A-Z^4 (Z4 blank) pp 2 VII, 1-171
$Wing^2$ M2679
Bound in with his A plain exposition...of the Prophet Daniel, 1681 (249)

MUSCULUS, Andreas

251 (Locorum communium theologicorum ex patribus ac ecclesiae orthodoxis collectorum)
[Erphordiae, Conradis Dreher excud.] [1568] Fol.
In two parts:
1. Tomus primus
☞, A-Z, Aa-Vv^{6} (Vv6 blank) Xx-Yy^{6} ff[4] 1-257[12]
Imperfect, wants ☞1 and 2, f257 numbered 357
2. Tomus secundus
*, Aaa-Zzz, 4A-4N^{6}, 4O^{8} ff[4] 1-210 [14]
Adams M2005 has ** for *.
Title page of part two on *1 recto is dated 1573
Binding Old. 948 and 442 on oak, 301x186

MUSCULUS, Wolfgang (1497-1563)

252 In apostoli Pauli ambas epistolas ad Corinthios commentarii.
Basileae, per Sebastianum Henricpetri, [1600] Fol.
α^{6} β^{8} a-z, A-S^{6} pp[28] 1-487
Not in Adams
Bound in with his In epistolam... ad Romanos commentarii, 1600 (255)

253 In D. Ioannis Apostoli Euangelium commentarii.
Basileae, ex officina Heruagiana per Eusebium Episcopium, 1580 Fol.
α^{4} a-z, A-Z, Aa-Nn^{6} pp[4] 1-165 [43]
Adams M2028
Binding Old. 449 (R.B.). 335x213

254 In Divi Pauli epistolas ad Philippenses Colossenses Thessalonicenses ambas & primam ad Timotheum commentarii...
Basileae, ex officina Heruagiana per Eusebium Episcopium, 1578 Fol.
a-z, A-M^{6}
Adams M2033
Bound in with his In Epistolas ad Galatas & Ephesios, 1569 (256)

255 In Epistolam D. Apostoli Pauli ad Romanos commentarii.
Basileae, per Sebastianum Henricpetri, (1600) Fol.
α^{6} β, γ^{4} A-V^{6} X,Y^{4} Z^{6} Aa$^{6-1}$ (A5 blank) pp[28] 1-278
Adams M2031
Signed John Scar[borough]
Also bound in : In apostoli Pauli ambas epistolas ad Corinthios commentarii, 1600 (252)
At back, two free end papers from 12mo sheets (folded but not sewn) from Petrus Ramus : Dialecticae. No signature, but p96 included. Not in BL.
Calf on board. 354x212

256 In epistolas Apostoli Pauli ad Galatas & Ephesios commentarii
Basel, Eusebius Episcopius (ex. off. Heruagiana),1569 Fol.
In two parts:
1. *^{4} a-t^{6} pp[8] 1-228
2. A-R^{6} pp[2] 3-173 [31]
Adams M2038
Also bound in : In Divi Pauli epistolas ad Phillipenses commentarii...,1578 (254)
Calf on board. 321x210

257 [In Esaiam prophetam commentarii]
Basileae, ex officina Heruagiana per Eusebium Episcopium, 1570 Fol.
α^{4} a-z, A-Z, Aa-Zz^{6} AA^{8} pp[10] 3-829 [12]
Wants α1, rest of α damaged by cutting device from title page now missing.
Adams M2015
Repaired. 330x213

258 In Euangelistam Matthaeum commentarii tribus tomis digesti: quibus non solum singula quaeque exponuntur sed & quid singulis Marci & Lucae differentibus locis notandum sit, diligentur expenditur.
Basileae, ex officina Heruagiana per Eusebium Episcopium, 1578 Fol.
α^4 a-z, A^6 (A6 blank) B-S^6 T^8 (T8 blank) V-Z, Aa-Ll^6 pp[8] 1-662 [26]
Adams M2021
Binding Old. 449 (R.B.) on board, repaired. 350x216

259 In Mosis Genesim plenissimi commentarii.....
Basileae, apud haeredes Ioannis Heruagii, 1565 Fol.
α^4 a-z, A-Z, Aa-Zz, Aaa-Ddd^6 pp[8] 1-821 [23]
Adams M2008
Binding Old. 449 (R.B.) on new board. 347x216

260 [In Psalterium commentarij.]
[Basel, Joannes Hervagius, 1563] Fol.
α, a-z, A-Z, aa-zz, AA-ZZ, 3A-3L^6 pp[6] 1-1181 [51]
Imperfect, wants α1, 5, 6 and all after 3L1
Adams M2010 gives pp1191
Rebound in doeskin. 320x205

261 Loci communes sacre theologiae.
Basileae, ex officina Heruagiana per Eusebium Episcopium, 1567 8°
α, a-z, A-Z, Aa-Zz, AA-YY^8 pp[16] 1-1406 [48]
Text in italic
Adams M2042
Calf on board. 193x125

NICEPHORUS, Callistus (Xanthopulus) (c.1256-1335)
262 Ecclesiasticae historiae libri decem & octo.
Basilieae, per Iohannes Operinum & Heruagium, 1560 Fol.
a-z, Aa-Zz, Aaa-Kkk^6 Lll^4 Mmm,Ooo^6 Ppp^8 pp[5] 6-956 [42]
p956 numbered 965. Leaves a1-a4 damaged
Adams N217
Calf on oak, repaired. Chained. 381x249

NICHOLAS de LYRA (c.1270-1349)
Postilla.
See Biblia Latina (41)

NOVARINI, Luigi (NOVARINUS, Aloysius)
263 Adagia ex sanctorum patrum ecclesiasticorumque scriptorum monumenter prompta....
(Lugduni, Laurentius Durand, 1637) Fol.
π^2 †, ††, 3†^{6} 4†^{2} A-Z, Aa-Hh^6 Ii^4 Kk, Ll^6 Mm^8 pp[44] 1-378 [42]
NN 0344616
Calf on board, repaired. Chained. 358x231

ORIGEN (ORIGENES ADAMANTIUS) (c.185-c.254)
264 Opera omnia quae extant... [Ed. Erasmus]
Apud inclytam Basileam ex officina Frokeniana, 1536 Fol.
In two volumes:
264.1 Prima parta
α-β, a-z, aa-zz, aaa-fff^6 pp[24] 1-899
Prefaced with Life by Erasmus
Rebound 1894 in doeskin. 337x230
264.2 Secunda parta
aa-zz, 3a-3z, 4a-4y^6 4z^8 pp 789 [44]
Wants aa
Adams O283 (both volumes)
Signed : liber Nicolai Arsent (?) emptus oxon pretium xs
Calf on oak, repaired. Chained. 338x222
Binding Old. 46 (W.G.)

PEARSON, John Bishop of Chester (1613-1686)

265 An exposition of the Creed. 10th edition
London, printed by W.Bowyer for J. Nicholson (and others), 1740 Fol.
π^{2}A-Z, Aa-Zz, Aaa-Fff^{4} (Fff4 blank) pp[8] 1-398 [10]
Title page ruled in red by hand
Signatures of three owners, one deleted
libris ----- ex aede Xti oxon 1744
G. Boraston 1879
Bernard Hancock 1880
Chichester Theological College
[Hancock was Vicar of Grantham 1917-1928]
Calf on board. 332x210

PETER LOMBARD (1110-1160)

266 Sacratissima sententiarum totius theologie quadripartita volumina.
Venetiis, per Gregoriam de Gregorius, 1514 Fol.
One part only of four
1-8^{8} ff[1] 2-64
First part of Adams P897
Bound in with DUNS SCOTUS : Tabula generalis, 1516 (104)

267 Sententiam libri IIII Quinta editio
Louanii, ex officina Bartholomaei Gravij, 1566 4°
A*-C*, a-z, A-Z, Aa-Tt, AAa-EEe^{4} pp[24] 1-520 [40]
Adams P911
Calf on board, repaired. 245x164

PHILO JUDAEUS (Philonius Alexandrini) (born c.15 B.C.E.)

268 Libri antiquitatem.
Basilieae, per Adamum Petrum, 1527 Fol.
α^{4} a-s^{4} pp[8] 1-142
Adams P1031
Bound in with CLEMENT : Opera, 1527 (86)

PINTO, Heitor (Hector Pintus) (1528-1584)

269 Commentaria in Danielem Nahum& Threnos Ieremiae.
Antuerpiae, ex officina typographicam Martin Nutij, 1598 8°
-6, A-Z, Aa-Zz, 3A-3F^{8} 3G^{2} ff[48] 1-414 [2]
Bibliothèque Nationale copy is A22448
Calf on board, repaired. 177x05

270 In Ezechielem prophetam commentaria.
Antuerpiae, in aedibus Petri Belleri, 1582 4°
*, A-Z, Aa-Zz, 3A-3Z, 4A-4G^{4} pp[8] 1-536 [72] + 10 leaves not numbered
NBi 0037075. Not in Adams.
The final 10 leaves (4E3/4 4F-4G^{4}) are Elenchus in Evangelis...ex comm F. Hectoris Pinti...in Ezechielem (Colophon: Daniel Veruliet,1582)
[See N Bi 0037073]
Calf on board, repaired. 247x164

PLINY (PLINIUS SECUNDUS, Gaius) (23-79)

271 [Naturalis hystoriae libri xxxij]
[Parrhisijs, Nicolae de Pratis, 1514] Fol.
aa, bb, cc^{6}, c-z, &, A-I^{8} K^{6} L^{8} ff[20] I-CCLXII
Imperfect, wants aa, bb,L
Adams P1553
No covers. 285x215

PLOWDEN, Edmund (1518-1585) Sergeant-at-Law

272 [Les comentaries, ou les reportes de E.P. de dyvers causes esteant matters de ley]
(London, Richard Tottel, 1579) Fol.
Begins Paschal 12 Eliz. I: Le briefe report del opinions del Iustices del commenbanke...
A-Z, AA-SS^4 TT^6 ff 403-565
STC as (273)
Also bound in : Vn report fait per vn vncerteine (sic) authour, 1588 (273)
No covers. 290x198

273 Vn report fait per vn vncerteine (sic) authour del part de vn argument del Edmond Plowden de Milieu Temple.
(London, Richard Tottel) 1588
A-D^4 (A1 blank) ff 1-15
STC^2 20046.3 A2 recto has Henry Bridgȝ
Bound in with : Les comentaries, 1579 (272)

PLUTARCH (46-120)

274 The Lives of the Noble Grecians and Romaines compared together by that Grave Learned Philosopher and Historiographer Plutarke of Chaeronea. Translated... into English by Sir Thomas North, Knight.
London, Richard Field, 1612 Fol.
A^8 B-Z, Aa-Zz, 3a-5n^{6}5p^8 pp[14] 1-1244 [32]
STC^2 20069
On back end paper: Ex dono Willielmi Petty 1742
On t.p : Johes Rowell
On front end paper : John Scarborough Grantham 1751
Thomas Scarborough
Parish Clerk Grantham 1751
Delivered this book 4 October 1816
John Logic
Light brown calf on board, gold tooling, edges formerly red. Repaired. 336x223

POLYBUS

De salubri victus ratione privatorum
(see GALEN : De plenitudine, 1528 (151))

POWER

275 The power of the Christ of God.
London, printed by R. Cotes for Jo: Bellamie and Ralph Smith, 1641 4°
*, A-G^4 pp[16] 1-46
Not in Wing
Bound with : An answer out of the West, 1667 (11)

RABANAS

See HRABANUS

RAINOLDS, John

276 De Romanae ecclesiae idololatria in cultus anctorum, reliquiarum, imaginum, aquae, salis, olei, aliarurmq[ue] rerum consecratorum, et sacramenti Eucharistiae operis inchoati libri duo
Oxoniae, apud Josephum Barnesium, 1596 4°
¶, A-Z, Aa-Rr^8 Ss^4 pp[14] 1-646
STC^2 20606
Bound in with WHITAKER : Disputatio de Sacra Scriptura, 1588 (334)

RASTELL, John

See FITZHERBERT : La Table, 1565 (148)

[RAWORTH, John]

277 Satisfaction concerning mixt communions vnsatisfactory....(animadversions upon a late book)
Satisfaction concerning mixt communions.
London, printed for Henry Overton, 1643
$A\text{-}B^4$ pp[2] 1-14
Wing S727
Printed at end : Imprimatur John Bachiler
Bound with : An answer out of the West, 1667 (11)

RAVISIUS, Johannes (Tixier, Jean, Seigneur de Ravisy) (d.1524)

278 Cornucopia Textoris; Officina Textoris.
[Paris, Reginald Chaudière, 1532] ? Fol.
Fragments only
i, (-i1, i8), l-o, r-z, &, , $aa\text{-}tt^8$ yy3-yy6 only
Wants all but ff 11-71, 81-112, 129-351, 371-374
Not in Adams.
Could be Catalogue Général de la Bibliothèque Nationale X1124.
No covers. 330x220

REFLECTIONS

279 Some reflections upon a discourse called Omnia à Belo comesta, containing some animadversions from the North upon a letter out of the West.
London, printed 1668 4°
$A\text{-}E^4$ F^2 (F2 blank) pp 1-41
Not in Wing
Bound with : An answer out of the West, 1667 (11)

RHODIGINUS, Ludovicius Caelius (1450-1520)

280 [Lectionem antiquarium libri XVI]
Basileae, apud Ioannem Frobenium, (1517) Fol.
$\alpha^8\beta\text{-}\delta$, aa^6 bb^8 a-z, A-Z, $2A\text{-}4C^6$ pp[80] 1-862
Imperfect, wants α1. Woodcut initials 5 or 8 lines, some marginalia
Not in Adams.
Binding Old. 951 with 979 on oak, repaired. Chained. 325x217

RIBERA, Francis (1537-1592)

281 In librum duodecim prophetarum commentarii.
Coloniae Agrippinae, in officina Birckmannica, sumptibus Arnoldi Mylii, 1593 Fol.
$a\text{-}h^6$ i^4 A-Z, Aa-Zz, $Aaa\text{-}Vvv^6$ Xxx^8 pp[103] 1-807
Adams R473
Binding Old. 449 on board, repaired. Chain scars. 310x195

RIVERIUS, Lazarus (1589-1655) (Lazaire Rivière)

282 The Practice of Physick in seventeen several books...to which are added: four books of.....Lazarus Riverius...unto which is a fifth book...of John Fernelius (Trans. N. Culpeper)
London, for George Sawbridge, 1678 Fol.
In two parts:
1. $A\text{-}4C^4$ $4D^6$ pp 644
2. $A\text{-}3E^4$ $3F^6$ pp 46 [30]
Wing R1564
Plain calf on board. 309x199

ROSINUS, Joannes Bartholomaeus (1551-1626)

283 Romanorum antiquitatum libri decem.
Basileae, ex officina haeredum Petri Pernae, 1583 Fol.
)(,)()(, a-z, $A\text{-}Y^6$ Z^8 pp[24] 1-49 [64]
Adams R798;)(3 recto ends incedetes via om-
Imperfect, wants Z8. Contains woodcuts and plan of military camp.
Calf on board, some leather ties. Chain re-rivetted. 235x212

ROUS, Francis (b.1615)

284 Archeologicae Atticae libri septem. Seven books of the Attic antiquities. Fifth Edition.
Oxford, A. Lichfield and H. Hall for John Adams and Edw. Forrest, 1658 4°
¶, A-Z, Aa-Zz, 3A-3B^{4}3C^2 pp[4] 1-374 [14]
Wing R2035
Bound in with GODWIN : Moses and Aaron, 1655 (154)

SADEEL, Antonius Chandeus (Antoine de le Roche de Chandieu) (1534-1591)

285 Opera theologica quae ipso adhuc vivente tuerunt edita.
[Heidelberg], in officina Sanctandreana, 1593 4°
*^{4} a-z, A-Z, Aa-Mm^8 (Mm 8 blank) aa-dd^4 ee^2 pp[8] 1-926 [36]
Adams L212
Motto on t.p. Ars longa : vita brevis
Calf on board, repaired. Chained. 254x172

SARPI, Paolo (Pietro SOAVE, pseud.) (1552-1623)

286 Historia del concilio tridentino. Seconda editione riveduta e corretta dall' autore.
1629 4°
No imprint, but printer's device copies Aldine dolphin on anchor.
π, t^4 tt^2 A-Z, Aa-Zz, 3A-3Z, 4A-4Z, 5A-5O^4 (5O3, 4 blank) pp[13] 1-842
Some notes on back end paper in Italian.
NS 0136444 gives [Geneva]
Bound vellum with 'yapp' edges. Title on spine. 228x175

SENECA, Lucius Annaeus (c.4 B.C.-65 A.D.)

287 Opera quae extant omnia [Edition of C.S. Curio, edited by Vincentius Prallius]
Basileae, ex officina Heruagiana per Eusebium Episcopium, 1573 Fol.
α^{10} a-z, A-Z, Aa-Cc^6 Dd^8 pp[20] 1-582 [20]
Adams S887
Calf on board, originally with ties. Chain scars. 324x216

SERRANUS, Petrus

288 Commentaria in Ezecheliem.
Antuerpiae, ex officina Christophori Plantini, 1572 Fol.
†^{2} A-Z, Aa^6 Bb^2 *^{4} pp[4] 1-289 [10]
Adams S996
Bound in with his In Leuitici lib. commentaria, 1572 (289)

289 In Leuitici lib. commentaria.
Antuerpiae, ex officina Christophori Plantini, 1572 Fol.
π^1 a-y^6 z^2 (z2 blank) pp[2] 1-264 [6]
Adams S994
Back end paper signed Steph Luddington [vicar of North Grantham 1591-1608] and (in same hand) Tho. Deane [vicar of South Grantham 1607-1625]
Calf on board. Chain scars. 344x325
Also bound in : Commentaria in Ezecheliem, 1572 (288)

[SEYMOUR. Thomas]

290 The case of interest, or usury, by T.S.
London, printed for Samuel Richards, bookseller in Nottingham, 1673 4°
A-E^4 F(-F2 blank ?) pp[2] 1-37 [1]
Not edition of Wing S2830
Bound with : An answer out of the West, 1667 (11)

SHERLOCK, Paul, S.J. (SHERLOGUS) (1595-1646)

291 Anteloquia cogitationem in Salomonius Canticorum Canticum historica simui & concionatoria...
[Second Edition]
Lugduni, sumptib. Jacobi and Petr. Prost, 1637-40 Fol.
In three volumes:

291.1 Anteloquia
π^1 ã^8 ẽ, ĩ õ^6 ũ^4 (ũ^4 blank) A-Z, AA-ZZ^6 (ZZ6 blank) pp[60] 1-532 [16]
Imperfect, wants a1. π^1 is binder's half title

291.2 Vestigatio I-XXIV
ã, a^8(-1) ẽ^6 ĩ^4 A-Z, Aa-Zz, AAa-VVv^6 (VVv6 blank) pp[36] 1-700 [82]
Calf on board. Chained. 361x228

291.3 Vestigatio XXV-XXXVII
¶, 2¶, 3¶, 4¶, 5¶, 6¶, 7¶, 8¶, 9¶^{4} A-Z, Aa-Pp^6 Qq-Zz, AAa-KKk^4 LLl^6 MMm-XXx^4 pp[72] 1-612 [90]
Imperfect, wants ¶1, ¶2; 5¶3/4 are signed ã3, ã4
¶¶2 verso is full plate engraving of Christ with angels.
All volumes NS 0499043
Calf on board. 361x228

SIGONIUS, Carolus (Pseud. of LAUREDANUS, Bernardus) (1524-1585)

292 Historium de occidentali imperio libri XX.
Basileae, ex officina (per) Thomae Guarini, 1579 4°
A-Z, Aa-Zz, AA-ZZ, 3A-3O^4 pp[2] 3-664 [34]
Adams S1118
Calf on board, repaired. 223x152

SKINNER, Stephen (1623-1667)

293 Etymologicon linguae Anglicanae.
Londini, typis T. Rycroft & prostant venales apud A. Brome (et al.), 1671
[A], B-D^4 E-V^2 Aa-Vv^4 Xx-Zz^2 3A-3Y^4 3Z^6 4A-4Z, 5A-5V^4 5X^2 404 leaves not numerated
Wing S3947
Calf on board, red label on spine : Skinneri Lexicon, 324x203
Presented by Dr. Babbington of Boothby Pagnell
Also signed : Barbara Topp 1686, Burnett

SMALRIDGE, George (Bishop of Bristol) (1663-1719)

294 [Sixty sermons preached on several occasions published from the originals (by Mary Smalridge)]
(London, William and John Innys, 1725) Fol.
[π] †^{2} *-5*, a-e, A-7Q^2 pp[42] 1-616
Wants t.p. π
Calf on board, gold-tooled on spine, red leather label. Chained. 411x244
On back free end paper
Ex Dono Johannis Brownlowe
Vicecomiti(s) Tyrconnel

SONCINUS (SOCINUS), Marianus the Elder (1482-1556)

295 Repetitio capituli [']sententiam sanguinis['] super materia irregularitatis.
[Naples, Jodocus Hohenstein c.1476] Fol.
26 leaves, without signatures or numeration, the first 6-line initial blank in [S]ententiam
Indice generale degli incunaboli delle biblioteche d'Italia (1972) No. 9074.
One other copy recorded, at Biblioteca Capitolare, Atri.
Bound in with LANFRANC de ORIANO : Repetitiones disputationes necnon tractatus diversorum doctorum, 1472 (202)

SPANHEIM, Friedrich (SPANHEMIUS) (1632-1701)

296 Dubia evangelica in tres partes distributa.
Geneva, sumptibus Petri Chouët, 1651 4°
This edition is two parts, issued separately and bound together:
1. Pars prima
*, **, a-Z, Aa-Yy^4 Zz^2 pp[16] 1-338 [26]
NS 0794584
2. Pars secundo
[Geneva?] sumptibus Iacobus Chouët, 1639
*, **, ¶^{4} ¶¶^{2} A-Z, Aa-Zz, 3A-3Z, 4A-4Z, 5A^4 5B^2 pp[28] 1-695 [52]
NS 0794588
Signed on back free end paper : Henry Saunders
Calf on board. 232x163

SPARROW, Anthony (1612-1685)

297 A rationale upon the book of Common Prayer.
London for T. Garthwait, 1668 12mo
π^2 A-T^{12} (T12 blank) pp[24] 1-408 [22]
NS 0797389
Variation Wing S4831, which is Timothy Garthwait.
Signed : (?) Allenson .M. Coll. Jes :Cant: 1706
Charles Boddington, Lichfield, 1899
Calf on board, covers now loose.
Presented by the Rev. S.I. Lee, Rector of Crowland, 1956
Also bound in ANDREWES, Lancelot : The forme of consecration, 1663 (9)

[SPEED, John] (1552-1629)

298 [The genealogies recorded in the sacred scriptures...by J.S]
No imprint
A-D^4 F^2 pp 1-34 [4]
Imperfect, wants A1, but see below (48)
STC^2 23039d
[Included in all Bibles (A.V.) printed for ten years after 1611 by patent issued to John Speed.]
Bound in with : Book of Common Prayer, Psalms and Bible 1634 (216)
There are also 3 leaves only (A1, F1/2) in : Bible (Norton and Bill) 1619 (48)
A1 is the title page for (298)

STELLA, Didacus (Diego de Estella) (1524-1578)

299 In evangelium secundum Lucam enarrationum.
Antuerpiae in aedibus Petri Belleri, 1593 Fol.
In two volumes bound together:
I Tomus primus
$*^8 {**}^{10}$ A-R^8 S^6 pp[36] 1-282 [1]
Imperfect, several leaves missing.
II Tomus secundus
A-V^8 (V8 blank) pp[2] 3-318
Imperfect, several leaves missing.
Adams S1705
In poor condition but repaired. 339x209

STEPHANUS, Henricus [I] (1460 - 1520)

300 Concordantiae Testamenti Noui, Graecelatine......
[Geneva] ex typographeio Henr. Stephani [II], 1594 Fol.
$(..)^4$ A-Z, AA-VV^6 XX^4 YY^6 pp[8] [2] 3-535
Adams S1756
Bequeathed by Francis Trigge, 1606
Binding calf on board, Old. 400 with 436, repaired. Chained. 356x219

STEPHANUS, Robertus, the Elder (1503 - 1559)

301 [Concordantiae Bibliorum vtriusque Testamenti Veteris et Novi]
[Paris] excudebat Robertus Stephanus in sua officina, 1555) Fol.
a-z, aa-zz, A-X^8 Y-Z^6 ff[2] 3-548
Imperfect, wants a1
Adams S1798
Calf on oak, repaired. Chained. 364x240

STEPHANUS de Caieta

302 Repetitio c. quoniam, in qua tractatur materia iuris patronatus.
[Naples, Jodocus Hohenstein, c.1476] Fol.
16 leaves without signatures or numeration, the first blank.
See Marco Santoro : La stampa a Napoli nel Quattrocento (Naples 1984) No. 272. No other copy located' (per D. E. Rhodes, British Library)
This is the only known copy.
Bound with LANFRANC de ORIANO : Repetitiones disputationes necnon tractatus diversorum doctorum, 1472 (202)

STERNHOLD, Thomas (d.1549) (with HOPKINS, John)

303 The whole booke of Psalms, collected into English meeter by Thomas Sternhold, John Hopkins and others, conferred with the Hebrew, with apt notes to sing them withall.
London, W.S[tansby] for the Company of Stationers, 1634 4°
A-G^8 pp[8] 1-90 [12]
STC^2 2649
Bound in with : Book of Common Prayer, 1634 (219)

304 The whole booke of Psalms collected into English metre, by Thomas Sternhold, John Hopkins and others.
London, for the Company of Stationers, 1682 12mo
A-D^{12} no pagination
Red rules inserted by hand.
Bound in with : Bible (J. Bill, T.Newcombe and Henry Hills), 1681 (50)

305 Another 12mo edition of above, 1730
Bound in with : Book of Common Prayer (T. Newcombe and H. Hills), 1711 (218)

306 The Whole book of Psalms: collected into English metre by Thomas Sternhold, John Hopkins and others: conferred with the Hebrew.
London, Printed by Freeman Collins for the Company of Stationers, 1708 4°
A-N^4 no pagination
Hand ruled in red
Bound in with : Book of Common Prayer (Baskett), 1715 (219)

307 The whole book of Psalms: collected into English metre by Thomas Sternhold, John Hopkins and others. Conferred with the Hebrew.
London, Printed by Freeman Collins for the Company of Stationers, 1737 12mo
A-N^{12} no pagination
Bound in with : Book of Common Prayer (Baskett), 1737 (220)

SURIUS, Laurentius (1521-1597)

308 In quatuor tomos conciliorum omnium tum generalium tum provincialum.
Coloniae Agrippinae, apud Geruvinum Calenium & haeredes Iohannis Quentelii, 1567 Fol.
In four volumes:

308.1 Index
a-k^4 **l^6 (**l6 blank) pp 92
Tomus primus
A^{*6} a-xxx^6 yyy-zzz^4 pp[16] 1-819

308.2 Tomus secundus
A*^{4} A-4T^6 pp [8] 1-89

308.3 Tomus tertius
A*^{2} A-4H^6 4I^4 (4I4 blank) pp[4] 1-930

308.4 Tomus quartus
a^2 *a-*z, *aa-*oooo^6 *pppp^4 pp[2] 1-1003
Adams C2772
Calf on board, repaired, small gold tooled motif of fleur de lys and monogram of HB on all four volumes. 351x230

SZEGEDIN, Stefan (Istvan Kis) (1505-1572)

309 Theologicae sincerae loci communes de Deo et homine perpetuis explicati....
Basileae, ex officina Pernea per Conradum VValdkirch, 1585 Fol.
α, β^6 γ^4 a-o^6 p^8 q-z, A-V^6 X^8 pp[32] 1-506 [24]
Adams S2225
Title page woodcut with compartment 160x100
One end paper is folio sheet from MARSILIIS, Hippolytus de : Opera. (Index only, no date)
Calf on board. 332x212

TACITUS, Cornelius (c.56 -c.120)

310 The Annales [and other works] Trans. R. Greenway, Fifth edition.
(London, printed by John Bill, 1622) Fol.
Four Books in two parts:
1. The Annales, The description of Germany
$¶^4$ A-Y^6 Z^4 pp[6] 1-227
Imperfect, wants ¶1
2. The end of Nero, the historie, the life of Agricola
$¶^6$ A-V^6 (V6 blank) pp[6] 1-12, 1-227
STC^2 23647
End paper signed Thomas Scarborough, Parish Clerk and Registrar
of Grantham, September 19, 1747 Endorsed January 1751
On back free end paper Ex Dono William Petty Grantham, his gift to the Library in the year 1742,
January the 13th 1751 (inserted by Scarborough)
Calf on board, repaired. 296x198

TERTULLIANUS, Q. Septimus (c.160-230)

311 Opera.
Basileae, in officina Frobeniana, 1528 Fol.
AA^6 BB^4 a-z, A-Z, Aa-Ll^6 Mm^4 a, b^6 pp[20] 1-692 [22]
Adams T406
Some marginalia. Parchment tags to sections.
Signed :Ex dono Ca(nonic)i Thome Robertsoni
Viue momor lati huc Raynoldi
Sclaterus (?)
Binding Old. 533 with 959 on oak boards, repaired. 325x215

312 De pallio liber, cum notis Francisci Iunii.
Lugduni Batavorum, ex officina Plantiniana apud Franciscum Raphalengium 1595 4°
A-K^4 pp[2] 3-73 [7]
Adams T419
Bound in with JUNIUS : Lectiones in Ionam, 1594 (196)

THEODORET (Blessed) Bishop of Cyrus(c.393-c.458)

313 Opera in duos tomos distincta.
Coloniae Agrippinae sumptibus viduae et haeredum Ioannis Stelsil (apud Ioannem Birkmannum),
1573 Fol.
In two parts:
1. Tomus prior
α^2, β^6, γ^4 δ^4 a-z, Aa-Zz, 3A-$3V^6$ pp[16] 1-791
2. Tomus alter
a1, b^6 a2,c^6 a-z, aa-zz, 3a-$3g^6$ pp[14] 1-634
Adams T481
Binding Old.449 with 835 on oak. Chained. 362x222

THUCYDIDES (c.455-401 B.C.)

314 [The hystory writtone by Thucidides.....(trans. by T. Nicolls)]
[London, W.Tylle, 1550] Fol.
[?] G-Z, Aa-Gg^6
Very imperfect, wants all before G, only H1/5 and M1/2 after Gg.
STC^2 24056
No covers, in bad condition. 204x195
Signed : Anne Grant, T.S. 1754. Margins filled with 18th Century graffiti (doggerel, exercises in
arithmetic, accounts)

[TORSHELL,Samuel] (1604 - 1650)

315 A case of conscience concerning flying in times of trouble.
London, printed for John Bellamie & Ralph Smith, 1643 4°
A-B^4 pp 1-15 [1]
Wing T1934
Signed : 'this book to me Dr. Raynor'
Bound with : An answer out of the West, 1667 (11)

On last blank page 'for Mr. Raynor this'

TRUXILL (TRUGILLO), Thomas de
316 Thesauri concionatorum. Postreme editio.
Lugduni, apud Carolum Pesnot, 1584 Fol.
Two volumes bound together:
I Tomus primus
*,**, A-Z, Aa-Zz, AA-PP^{6} (PP6 blank) pp[24] 1-635 [96]
II Tomus secundus
*, a-z, A-Z, Aa-Zz, AA-[GG^{6} HH^{4} II^{6} KK^{4}]a, b^{6} [c^{4}] pp 1-940 [24]
Adams T1009
Title page in red and black
Very imperfect, many sections and pages missing.
Calf on board, Old. 601. 381x342

TUDESCHI, Nicolaus (Niccolò de') (Nicolaus de Sicilia, Abbot, Palermo) (1386-1445)
317 Concilium [Accessit] Quaestiones et disputationes.
Lugduni, per Nicolaum de Benedictis, 1507 Fol.
In three parts:
1. Prima pars conciliorum
a^{4} b-h^{8} i^{6} ff[4] I-LX
2. Secunda pars conciliorum
A-I^{8} K^{10} ff[8] I-LXXIIII
3. Quaestiones et disputationes
aa-ee^{6} ff[1] II-XXIX
Not in Adams, but see BMC VIII, 256 (dated 1500)
Signed Rich. Hall (16th century hand) also Peter Arkland, Robert Bransby, Francis Handsford.
Bound with slips of vellum MS in red, blue and black. End papers (now free) are leaves of a legal treatise on inheritance, 60 lines 2 cols gothic (270x63) signature b, blank initials on b1 [N. Italian 15th century]
Calf on oak. Binding Old. 556 with 959. 430x295

TYTH-GATHERERS
318 Tyth-Gatherers no Gospel Officers.
Printed in the Hopefull-yeare both of Civill and Christian Liberty, 1646 4°
A-D^{4} pp[8] 1-21
Wing T3600
Bound with : An answer out of the West, 1687 (11)

URSINUS, Sacharias(1539-1583)
319 Tractationum theologicarum volumen secondum.
Neustadii Palatinorum, 1589 [Printer's device, Harnisch] Fol.
*, **^{6}***^{4} ****^{6} (****6 blank) A-Z, Aa-Zz, 3A, 3B^{6} 3C^{8} 3D-3G^{6} 3H^{8} (3H7 blank, -3H8) pp[44] 1-652
Imperfect, wants page 652.
Adams U85
Calf on board, poor condition, repaired. 328x200

VERGILIUS, Polydorus (1470 - 1555)
320 Anglicae Historiae libri XXVI
[Basileae, apud Io. Bibelium, 1534] Fol.
a-z, A-Z, Aa-Hh^{6} [Ii]^{6} pp 1-600 [10]
Imperfect, wants lower part of title page and Ii, some marginalia damaged by trimming.
Adams V446
First page of text enclosed in four woodcut borders. At the head a fox carrying off a hen is chased off by peasants with flails, hoes and spades.

VERMIGLI, Pietro Martire (Peter Martyr) (1500-1562)
321 In D. Pauli Apostoli Priorem ad Corinthios Epistolam. Editio secunda.
Tiguri, apud Christophrum Froschouerum, 1579
aa, a-z, A-Q^{6} R^{8} *^{6} **^{4} ***^{6} (***6 blank) ff[6] 1-242 [15]
Adams M790
Calf on board, repaired. Chain scars. 317x203

322 In duos libros Samuelis prophetae qui vulgo priores libri Regum appellantur
Tiguri, excudebat Christophorus Froschouerus, 1575 Fol.
aa-cc, a-z, A-Z, Aa-Hh^6 Ii^4 Kk^6 (kk6 blank) ff[13] 1-333
Adams M778
Calf on board. Cambridge binding by Thomas Thomas, (No 53 in Oldham: Shrewsbury School Library Bindings, 1943).
Repaired. 325x200

323 In epistolam S. Pauli apostoli ad Romanos.
Basileae, apud Petrum Pernam, 1558 Fol.
α^6 $*^4$ (*4 blank) a-z, A-Z,Aa-Gg^6 Hh^4 α-δ^6 pp[18] 1-643 [46]
*iii is signed a3
Adams M784
Vellum on board, gold tooled flowers on spine. Chained. 361x255

324 In primum librum Mosis commentarii...
Tiguri, excudebat Christophorus Froschouerus, 1579 Fol.
a-b, A-Z, Aa-Ii^6 Kk^8 (kk8 blank) ff[12] 1-199
Adams M771
Calf on Oak, Cambridge binding by Thomas Thomas (c.f. 322). Chain scars. 331x200

325 In Librum iudicum.
Tiguri, apud Christophorum Froschouerum, 1582 Fol.
α, β, γ, a-z, A-F^6 G^8 (G8 blank)β^8 (β8 blank) ff[18] 1-181 [8]
Adams M775 (omits β^8 at end)
Calf on board. Cambridge binding by Thomas Thomas (c.f. 322) repaired. 330x210

326 Melachim, id est Regum libri duo posteriores cum commentariis Petri Martyris.... in primum totum...et Ioannis VVolphii in secundi quatuordecim ultima capita.
Tigura, excudebat Christophorus Froschouerus, 1581 Fol.
*, **, aaa-ccc, a-z, A-Z, Aa-Zz,AA-EE^6 FF^8 (FF8 blank) ff[30] 1-451
The work of Johann Wolf begins at f282 verso
Adams M782
Calf on board bound with slips of vellum MS in English. 322x205

VIEGAS, Blasio
327 Commentaria exergetici in Apocalypsim Ioannis apostoli.
Lugduni, sumptibus Horatii Cardon, 1602 4°
*, A-Z, AA-ZZ, 3A-3Z, 4A-4Z, 5A-5Z, 6A-$6E^4$ $6F^2$ pp[8] 1-894 [76]
This edition not in BL, or NUC
Title page in red and black
Bequeathed by Francis Trigge, 1606
Plain calf on board. Chained. 255x175

VIGUERIUS, Johannes (fl.1558)
328 Ad naturalem et Christianam philosophiam institutiones... D.Thomae Aquinatis eruditione confirmatae....Opera atque....
Parisiis, (excudebat Guilielmus Thibout) apud Claude Fremy, 1555 Fol.
ã, $e^6 i^2$ a-z, A-Z, Aa-Bb^6 ff[14] 1-289
Two lines blind type on f289
Adams V766
Inscription : Emptus Lincolnia 1590 4 mense Feb
pretio 4s per me Guliel Straus (?)
artem magistrum mese Feb
Binding Old.859 (P.L.) on board, repaired. Chained. 333x203
Also bound in is HEGESIPPUS : De rebus a Iudaeorũ...., 1544 (170)

VINCENTIUS (Burgundus) Vincent de Beauvais (d.1264)
329 Speculi maioris tomi quatuor.
Venetiis 1591 apud Dominicum Nicolinum Fol.
In four volumes:

329.1 Tomus primus: tota naturalis historia.
a^4 (a4 blank) a^6 b^4 a^6 b^8 AB^6 C^4 D-Z, Aa-Zz, Aaa-Ggg^8 ff[27] 1-424

329.2 Tomus secundus: qui speculum doctrinale inscribitur.
π1 $a^6$$\pi$2 (blank) b^{10} (b10 blank) a, b^6 ^{4} A-$K^8$$L^6$ M-Z^8 Aa-Nn^8 Oo^{10} ff[16] 1-298

329.3 Tomus tertius: qui speculum morale inscribitur.
a^8 (a7, a8 blank) A^4 A-Z, Aa-Mm^8 ff[10] 1-280

329.4 Tomus quartus: qui speculum historiale inscribitur.
a^8 (a8 blank) b^6 d^8 a^{10} (a10 blank) A-Z, Aa-Zz Aaa-Kkk^8 Lll^6 Mmm-Ppp^8 Qqq^6 ff[32] 1-491
All Adams V811. Collation of preliminaries differs in vol. 4
Calf on board, repaired. 334x224

WALKER, John (Rector of St. Mary's the More, Exeter)(1674-1747)

330 An attempt towards recovering an account of the number and sufferings of the clergy of the Church of England ... in the late times of the Grand Rebellion.
London, by W. S. for J. Nicholson (et al.), 1714 Fol.
In two parts, bound together:
1. π^2 A-N, a-d, A-Z, Aa-Zz, Aaa-Eee^2 pp[2] i-li [14] 1-203
2. B-Z, Aa-Zz, 3A-3Z, 4A-4Z, 5A-$5R^2$ $5S^4$ pp 1-436
NW 0036438
On title page Ex dono Vir. Rev: John Golland A.M.
Bibliotecha Granthamiensis
Calf on board.Chained. 363x218

WECKER, Ioannes (1528-1586)

331 Antidotarum speciale.
Basileae per Eusebium Episcopium & Nicolai frat. haeredes, 1588 Fol.
$(:)^8$ a-z, A-R^6 S^4 T^6 pp[16] 1-475-[28]
Adams W33
Calf on board, repaired. Chain scars. 322x206

332 Medecinae utriusque syntaxes, ex Graecorum, Latinorum, Arabumque thesauris.
Lugduni, apud Stephanum Michaelum, 1583 Fol.
[*1] a^6 $*^2$ b-z, A-Z, Aa-Ss^6 Tt^8 pp[16] 1-752 [28]
NW 0143892. Cat. Wellcome Historical Medical Library 6708 agrees but gives apud B. Honorat
Calf on board, Cambridge binding by Thomas Thomas (c.f. 322). 354x225

WESENBECIUS, Matthaeus (1531-1586)

333 Paratitla in Pandectas iuris civilis ab authore recognita & aucta. Accesserunt prolegomena de finibus studiorum iuriprudentiae.
Basileae, 1568 (per Eusebium Episcopium et Nicolai fratris haeredes) Fol.
α, $\beta^6\delta^8$ a-z, A-V^6 X^8 pp[6] 7-542 [38]
Not in Adams.
Rebound. Trimming has damaged final letters of extensive marginalia. 336x215

WHITAKER, William (1548 - 1595)

334 Disputatio de sacra scriptura contra huius temporis papistas imprimis Robertum Bellarminum Iesuitam.....& Thoma Stapletonum.....
Cantabrigiae, ex off. T. Thomasii, 1588 4°
A, B^4 C-Z^8 Aa-Mm^8 (-Mm7, Mm8 blank) pp[8] 1-530 [10]
STC^2 25366
Calf on board. Chained.197x143
Also bound in RAINOLDS : De Romanae ecclesiae idolatria, 1596 (276)

335 [Praelectiones...in quibus tractatur controuersia de ecclesia.....]
[Cambridge, John Legat, 1599] 4°
)?(, A-K, Aa-Zz, 3A-3Z, 4A-$4S^4$ (4S4 blank) pp 1-668 [32]
Imperfect, wants title leaf)?(1
STC^2 25368
Half page of notes in shorthand (Shelton?) on back end paper.
Calf on board. 220x110

WHITGIFT, John (1614 -1672)

336 The defense of the aunswere to the Admonition against the Replie of T.C.[= Thomas Cartwright, c.f. STC^2 4711]
London, Henry Binnemann for Humphrey Toye, 1574 Fol.
a^4 b^8 A-Xxx^6 Yyy^4 $Aaaa^6$ pp[20] 1-812 [11]
STC^2 25430
Unsigned inscription on back end paper, also recipe 'Medecyne for the Ague' on verso of t.p.
Binding Old. 46(W.G.) with 795 (493), original calf on new oak board. 296x203

WILKINS,John

337 Ecclesiastes or a discourse concerning the gift of preaching.
London,printed by M. F. for Samuel Gellibrand, 1646 4°
A-N^4 pp[4] 1-108
Wing W2188
Bound with : An answer out of the West, 1667 (11)

WILLET, Andrew (1562-1621)

338 [Synopsis Papismi, that is a general view of Papistry. Now this third time perused and published.]
[London, Felix Kingston for Thomas Man, 1600] Fol.
[?] D-Y^6 Aa-4Z5A-$5E^6$ $5F^4$ pp[?] 1114 [28]
Imperfect, wants all before D
STC^2 25698
End papers are four leaves from CAMPEGIUS : Tractatus de testibus, et universa testimoniorum. (Cologne, Gymnicius, 1596)
Bequeathed by Francis Trigge, 1606
Wants covers. 321x224

WILLIAMS, Sir Roger (1540?-1595)

339 In obitum illustrisismi (sic) nobilissimique viri D. Roberti Dudlaei..carmina funebra.
London, T[homas] Orwinus, impensis J[ohn] Daldern, 1588
One broadsheet, imperfect.
STC^2 25733.5
Used as binder's end paper in HOSPINIANUS : De origine monachatus (149)

WOLF, Ambrose (pseud. of HERDESIANUS, Christoph, 1523-1585)

340 De fundamenta Lutheranae doctrinae de Vbiquitate...(with) De confessione Augustana....
No imprint, but dated 1585 4°
In two parts bound together:
1. De fundamenta lutheranae doctrinae
¶^{4} a-z, A-E^4 pp[8] 1-224
2. De confessione Augustana
Aa-Nn^4 pp[2] 3-104
Adams W228
Copy in Coll. Jes. Cantab. has stamped imprint Geneuae, apud Abdelem Riverium
Bound in with WOLF, Heinrich : Chronologia, 1585 (341)

WOLF, Heinrich (son of Johann)

341 [Chronologia sive de tempore et ejus mutationibus ecclesiasticis tractatio theologica.]
[Tiguri, in officina Froschouiana, 1585] 4°
aa^6 A-V^4 (V4 blank) pp[12] 1-156 [1]
Imperfect, wants aa1
Adams W230 (quotation on V3 recto has 6 lines)
Binding Old. 449 on oak, repaired. Chained. 205x142
'Grantham Library' on aa2 recto
Also bound in WOLF, Ambrose : De fundamenta Lutheranae doctrinae, 1585 (340)

WOLF, Johann (WOLPHIUS) of Zürich (1522-1571)

342 [Deuteronomium sermonum libri IIII.]
[Tiguri, apud Ioannem VVolphium F. typis Frosch., 1592] Fol.
$\alpha\beta^6$ g A-Z, a-c^6 (c6 blank) ff[16] 1-155
Imperfect, wants α, β
Adams W238
Rebound. 305x198
Also bound in : In sacram historiam Iosuae, 1592 (345) and In Esdrae librum primum, 1584 (343)

343 Esdras. In Esdrae librum primum....commentariorum lib. III.
Tiguri, excudebat Christoph. Froschouerus, 1584 Fol.
aa, bb^6 cc^4 A-X^6 Y^4Z^6 (Z6 blank) ff[16] 1-135
Adams W241
Bound in with his Deuteronomium sermonum libri IIII, 1592 (342)

344 Historia Iudicum quia morte Jehosuae usque ad Heli sacerdotem Israeli annos CCXCIX.
Tiguri, apud Iohannem VVolphium F. typis Frosch, 1598 Fol.
Aa^6 Bb^4 A-Y^6 Z^4 a^6 (a6 blank) ff[10] 1-141
Not in Adams
Plain calf on oak, repaired. Chain scars. 319x198
See also VERMIGLI : Melachim,1581 (326), which was completed by Wolf.

345 In sacram historiam Iosuae...sermonum liber unus.
Tiguri, apud Ioannem VVolphium F. typis Frosch, 1592 Fol.
a^6 b-c^8 A-I^6 K^8 (K8 blank) ff[24] 1-61
Adams W239
Bound in with his Deuteronomium sermonum libri IIII, 1592 (342)

346 Nehemias, sive in Nehemiae de instaurata Hierosolyma librum, qui secundus Esdrae dicitur, commentariorum libri tes.
Tiguri, excudebat Christophorus Froschouerus, 1570 Fol.
α^6 β^8 (β8 blank) a-v^6 x^4 y^6 (y6 blank) ff[13] 1-129
Adams W240 gives α^4
Plain calf on board. Chain scars. 318x206

ZANCHIUS, Hieronymus (1516-1590)

347 Compendium praecipuorum capitum doctrinae Christianae.
Neustadii in Palatinatũ, apud vid. VVilhelm Harnisii, 1598 8°
a^8 b^6 (b6 blank) A-Z, Aa-Ss^8 Tt^2 pp[26] 1-658 [1]
Adams Z34
Calf on oak, repaired. Chain scars. 174x105

348 .....De Incarnatione Filii Dei.
(Heidelbergae, ex officina Josuam Harnisch, 1593) 8°
¶, *, A-Z, Aa-Zz, Aaa-Iii^8 pp[30] 1-875
Calf on board, repaired 1894. Chain scars. 184x111
Adams Z36
Imprint torn from ¶1

349 De natura Dei, seu de divinis attributis, libri V.
Neustadii Palatinorum, apud viduam VVilhelmi Harnisii, 1598 4°
a-d^4 e^2 A-Z, Aa-Zz, 3A-3Z, 4A-4Z, 5A-$5K^4$ $5L^2$ pp[36] 1-767 [51]
Not in Adams or BL.
Back end papers sheets from 8° Picture Bible, Parts of Exodus signed K, K5 with quatrains in German (italic). Not identified.
Calf on board. Chain scars. 252x174

350 De operibus Dei intra spacium sex dierum.....Secunda editio
Hanoviae, sumptibus Iosuae & VVilhelmi Harnisiorum (apud Guilielmum Antonium), 1597 4°
a, b, A-Z, AA-ZZ, 3A-3Z, a-z, aa-zz, 3a-3z, 4a, $4b^4$ pp[16] 1-1081 [39] p 126 reads p 98
Adams Z40
Calf on board. Chain scars. 259x176

351 De tribus Elohim, aeterno Patre, Filio et spiritus sancto uno eodemque Jehova, libri XIII. In duas distincti partes.
Neustadii Palatinorum, typis Iosuae & VVilhelm Harnisiorum, 1597-98 4°
In two parts:
1. Pars prior
a-e, A-Z, Aa-Zz, 3A-3M^4 pp[40] 1-463
2. Pars altera (on t.p. Neustadt 1598)
[.·.]^4 3N-3Z, 4A-4Z, 5A-5D (5D5 blank) pp[8] 464-717 [48]
Adams Z48 does not distinguish parts.
Calf on board. Chain scars. 259x176

352 In D. Pauli Apostoli Epistolas ad Philippenses Colossenses Thessalonicenses....
Neostadii, excudebat Matthaeus Harnisius, 1594 Fol.
In two parts:
1. Ad Philippenses
(:)^6 ((:)6 blank), A-T^6 V^4 (V4 blank) pp[10] 1-233
2. Ad Colossenses & Thessalonicenses
a-o^6 p^4 (p4 blank) q-y^6 z^4 ^{4}(4 blank) pp 1-174 [6] 181-266 [6]
Adams Z50
Bound in with his In D. Pauli epistolam ad Ephesios, 1594 (353)

353 In D. Pauli epistolam ad Ephesios, commentarius
Neostadii, excudebat Matthaeus Harnisius,1594 Fol.
*^{6} **^{4} A-S (-S6 blank?), a-x^6 y^4 (-y4blank?) pp[20] 1-507
Adams Z51
Rebound. 338x205
Also bound in :In D. Pauli Apostoli epistolas ad Philippenses...., 1597 (352)

354 Miscellaneorum libri tres. Tertium nunc editi. De praedestinatione sanctorum.
Neapoli Palatinorum, excudebat Matthaeus Harnisius, 1592 Fol.
In two parts:
1. Miscellaneorum libri tres.
(:)^6 (:)(:), (:)(:)(:)^{4}A-Z, AA-DD^6 EE^4 (EE4 blank) pp[28] 1-330
2. De praedestinatione.
3A-3N^8 3P^6 3Q^4 pp 3-191
3A1(title leaf?) apparently not bound in : Adams Z54, (but part 2 has colophon Argentinae 1563)
Binding calf on board, repaired. 336x210

355 Tractationem theologicarum volumen librum de Operibus creationis proxime sequens: et priman tractatus de redemptione partem continens.
Neostadii Palatinatus, Iosuae & VVilhelmi Fratrum Harnisiorum, 1597 Fol.
*^{6} A-Z, Aa-Zz, 3A-3T^4 3V^6 3X^4 3Y^8 (Yyy8 blank) pp[12] 1-807 [23]
Adams Z57
Back end paper is sig. Z3.4, from [Muret : Aristotelis topicorum Lib. VII, Ingolstadt, A. Sartorius, 1603]
Calf on board. Chain scar. 344x207

ZWINGER, Theodor (1532-1588)

356 Theatrum humanae vitae.
Basileae, ex officina Episcopiorum, 1586-87) Fol.
Twenty four volumes bound as four, signed and foliated continuously:

365.1 Vols. I-III
*, **, ***, a-z, A-Z, Aa^6 Bb^8 (Bb8 blank) Cc-Zz, AA-TT^6 VV^{10} (VV10 blank) pp[40] 1-1087

356.2 Vols. IV-IX
XX-ZZ, aa-dd^{6}ee^8 ff-zz, aaa-sss^6 ttt^8 uuu-zzz, AAA-ZZZ, aAa-tTt^{6}uVu^8 (uVu8 blank) xXx-zZz^6 AaA-HhH^6 IiI^8 (-IiI8) pp 1089-2344
Imperfect, wants XX, YY, gGg and hHh interchanged

356.3 Vols. X-XVIII
KkK-YyY^6 ZzZ^8 aaaa-yyyy^6 zzzz^{10} AAAA-DDDD^6 EEEE^8 FFFF-KKKK^6 LLLL^8 MMMM-ZZZZ, aAAa-mMMm^6 nNNn^8 oOOo-zZZz, AaaA-GggG^6 HhhH^8 (HhhH8 blank) pp 2347-3466
Imperfect, wants KkK1

356.4 Vols XIX-XXIX
IiiI-TttT^{6} VvvV^{10} XxxX-ZzzZ, 5a-5s^{6} 5t^{8} 5u-5z^{6} (5z6 blank) 5A-5D^{6} 5E^{10} 5F-5H^{6} 5I^{4} 5K-5Z^{6} aaAaa^{6} bbBbb^{8} ccCcc-llLll^{6} mmMmm^{4} nnNnn^{6} ooOoo^{4} pp 3467-4373
Continues with unfoliated indexes etc.
ppPpp-ssSss^{6} ttTtt-yyYyy^{8} zzZzz^{10} AAaAA, BBbBB^{6} CCcCC^{8} DDdDD-XXxXX^{6} YYyYY^{8}
Adams Z215 (all volumes)
Bequeathed by Francis Trigge, 1606
Calf on board. Old. 594 (43) on 338.1, 338.2 (chained) and backcover only of 338.3. Repaired. 376x324
See also LYCOSTHENES, Conrad : Similium loci communes...cum T.Z. similitudinum methodo, 1575 (225)

DIVI IOANNIS

CHRYSOSTOMI

ARCHIEPISCOPI

CONSTANTINOPOLITANI

OPERVM

TOMVS SECVNDVS:

EA COMPLECTENS, QVÆ FACIVNT AD elucidationem Matthæi, Marci, & Lucæ, quatenus haberi potuerunt: quibus addita est breuis enarratio in Matthæum.

Horum inuenies catalogum proxima pagina.

PARISIIS,

M. D. LXXXVIII.

CVM PRIVILEGIO REGIS.

II. Cat. 83. St John Chrysostom: Opera. *Paris, 1588. Title page with device of the Great Ship (Photograph by David George)*

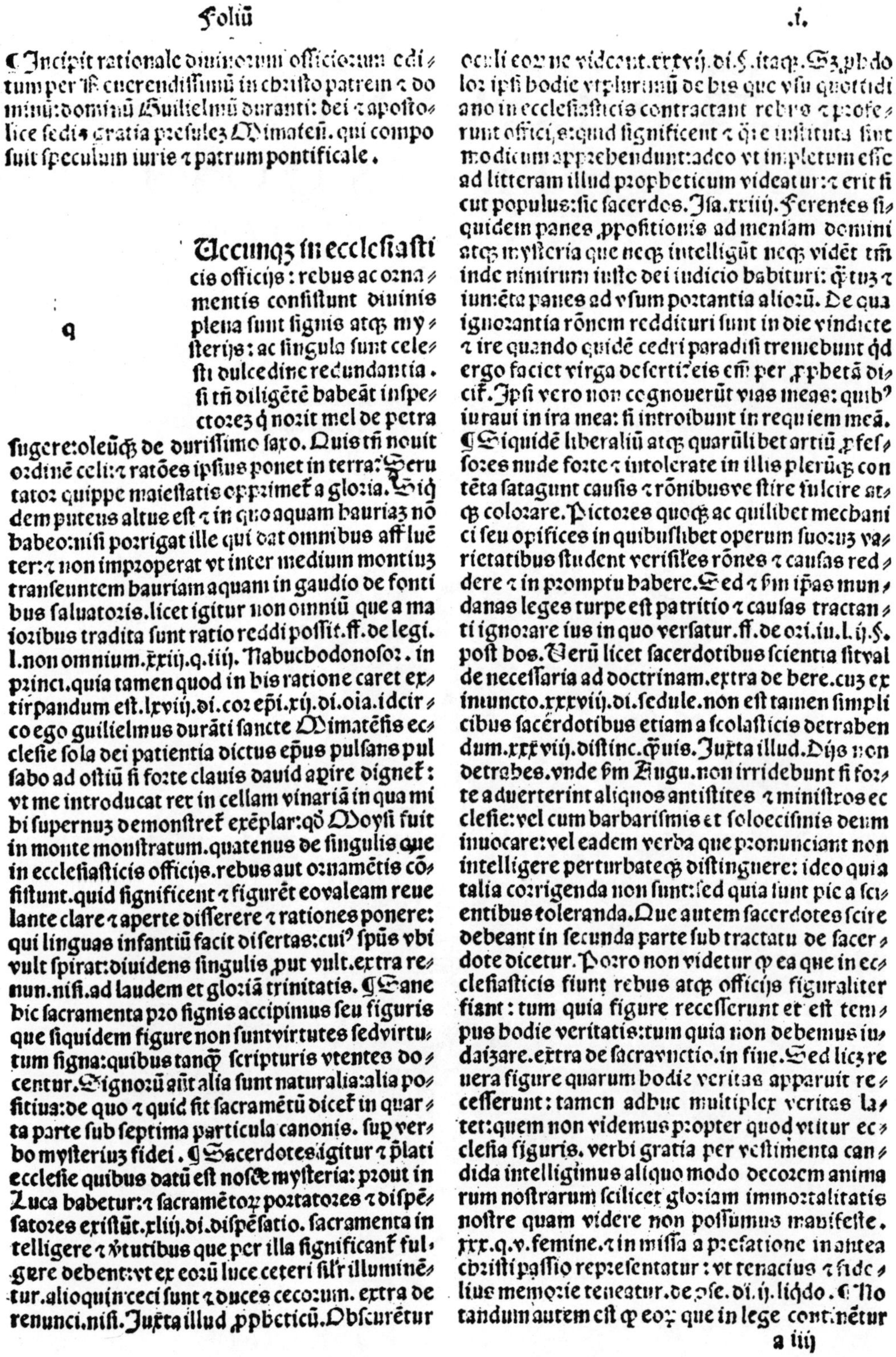

Foliū .i.

¶ Incipit rationale diuinorum officiorum editum per R. reuerendissimū in christo patrem et dominū: dominū Guilielmū duranti: dei et apostolice sedis gratia presulez Mimatenṡ. qui composuit speculum iuris et patrum pontificale.

Quecunq3 in ecclesiasticis officijs: rebus ac ornamentis consistunt diuinis plena sunt signis atq3 mysterijs: ac singula sunt celesti dulcedine redundantia. si tn̄ diligētē habeāt inspectorez q̄ norit mel de petra sugere: oleūq3 de durissimo saxo. Quis tn̄ nouit ordinē celi: et ratōes ipsius ponet in terra? Scrutator quippe maiestatis opprimetur a gloria. Siquidem puteus altus est et in quo aquam hauriaz nō habeo: nisi porrigat ille qui dat omnibus affluēter: et non improperat vt inter medium montiuz transeuntem hauriam aquam in gaudio de fontibus saluatoris. licet igitur non omniū que a maioribus tradita sunt ratio reddi possit. ff. de legi. l. non omnium. xxiij. q. iiij. Nabuchodonosor. in princi. quia tamen quod in his ratione caret extirpandum est. lxviij. di. cor epi. xij. di. oia. idcirco ego guilielmus durāti sancte Mimatēsis ecclesie sola dei patientia dictus epus pulsans pulsabo ad ostiū si forte clauis dauid apire dignetur: vt me introducat rex in cellam vinariā in qua mihi supernuz demonstretur exēplar: qd̄ Moysi fuit in monte monstratum. quatenus de singulis que in ecclesiasticis officijs. rebus aut ornamētis cōsistunt. quid significent et figurēt eo valeam reuelante clare et aperte disserere et rationes ponere: qui linguas infantiū facit disertas: cui⁹ spūs vbi vult spirat: diuidens singulis put vult. extra re. nun. nisi. ad laudem et gloriā trinitatis. ¶ Sane hic sacramenta pro signis accipimus seu figuris que siquidem figure non sunt virtutes sed virtutum signa: quibus tanq̄ scripturis vtentes docentur. Signorū aūt alia sunt naturalia: alia positiua: de quo et quid sit sacramētū dicetur in quarta parte sub septima particula canonis. sup verbo mysteriuz fidei. ¶ Sacerdotes igitur et plati ecclesie quibus datū est nosce mysteria: prout in Luca habetur: et sacramētorum portatores et dispēsatores existūt. xliij. di. dispēsatio. sacramenta intelligere et virtutibus que per illa significantur fulgere debent: vt ex eorū luce ceteri illuminētur. alioquin ceci sunt et duces cecorum. extra de renunci. nisi. Iuxta illud ppheticū. Obscurētur oculi eorum ne videant. xxxvij. di. §. itaq3. Sz ph dolor ipsi hodie vt plurimū de his que vsu quottidiano in ecclesiasticis contractant rebus et proferunt officijs: quid significent et q̄re instituta sint modicum apprehendunt: adeo vt impletum esse ad litteram illud propheticum videatur: et erit sicut populus: sic sacerdos. Isa. xxiiij. Ferentes siquidem panes ppositionis ad mensam domini atq3 mysteria que neq3 intelligūt neq3 vidēt tn̄ inde nimirum iuste dei iudicio habituri: q̄ tuz et iumēta panes ad vsum portantia aliorū. De qua ignorantia rōnem reddituri sunt in die vindicte et ire quando quidē cedri paradisi tremebunt qd ergo faciet virga deserti? eis enī per pphetā dicit. Ipsi vero non cognouerūt vias meas: quib⁹ iuraui in ira mea: si introibunt in requiem meā. ¶ Siquidē liberaliū atq3 quarūlibet artiū pfessores nude forte et intolerate in illis plerūq3 contēta satagunt causis et rōnibus vestire fulcire atq3 colorare. Pictores quoq3 ac quilibet mechanici seu opifices in quibuslibet operum suoruz varietatibus student verisiles rōnes et causas reddere et in promptu habere. Sed et sm ipas mundanas leges turpe est patritio et causas tractanti ignorare ius in quo versatur. ff. de ori. iu. l. ij. §. post hos. Verū licet sacerdotibus scientia sit valde necessaria ad doctrinam. extra de here. cuz ex iniuncto. xxxviij. di. sedule. non est tamen simplicibus sacerdotibus etiam a scolasticis detrahendum. xxxviij. distinc. q̄uis. Iuxta illud. Dijs non detrahes. vnde sm Augu. non irridebunt si forte aduerterint aliquos antistites et ministros ecclesie: vel cum barbarismis et soloecismis deum inuocare: vel eadem verba que pronunciant non intelligere perturbateq3 distinguere: ideo quia talia corrigenda non sunt: sed quia sunt pie a scientibus toleranda. Que autem sacerdotes scire debeant in secunda parte sub tractatu de sacerdote dicetur. Porro non videtur q̄ ea que in ecclesiasticis fiunt rebus atq3 officijs figuraliter fiant: tum quia figure recesserunt et est tempus hodie veritatis: tum quia non debemus iudaizare. extra de sacra vnctio. in fine. Sed licz re uera figure quarum hodie veritas apparuit recesserunt: tamen adhuc multiplex veritas latet: quem non videmus propter quod vtitur ecclesia figuris. verbi gratia per vestimenta candida intelligimus aliquo modo decorem animarum nostrarum scilicet gloriam immortalitatis nostre quam videre non possumus manifeste. xxx. q. v. femine. et in missa a prefatione in antea christi passio representatur: vt tenacius et fidelius memorie teneatur. de cōse. di. ij. liquido. ¶ Notandum autem est q̄ eorum que in lege continētur

a iiij

III. Cat. 105. Incipit of Duranti: Rationale divinorum officinorum, *Lyon, 1499.*
The only recorded copy of this edition in a British library
(Photograph by David George)

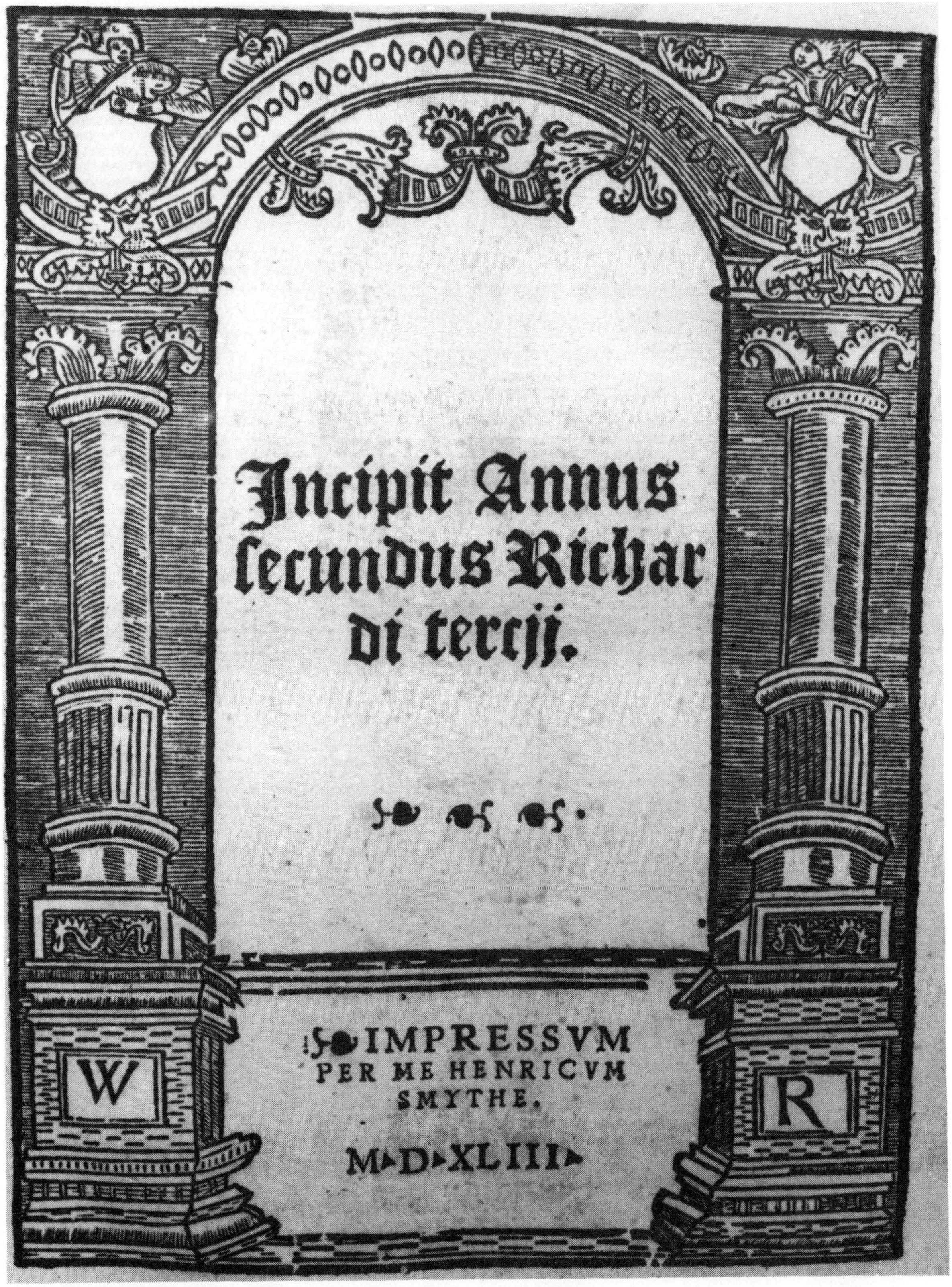

IV. Cat. 135. English Statutes Year Book, *2 Richard III, London, 1543. Not recorded in STC*
(Photograph by David George)

Glo.or. Ad Hebreos Ca. I Glo.or.

Incipit epl'a Pauli ad Hebreos.

Multifa- Ca. I

rie multisq3 modis olim de9 loquēs patribus in prophetis:

Nouissime dieb9 istis locut9 ē nobis in filio: quē cōstituit herēdē vniuersorum: per quem fecit & secula. Qui cum sit splendor glorie

Incipit postilla venerabilis patris/fratris Nicolai de Lyra super epistolam ad Hebreos. Ca. I

V. *Cat. 41.6. A page from* Textus Biblie cum glossa ordinaria (et) Nicolai de Lyra postilla, *Basel, 3 March 1508*
(Photograph by David George)

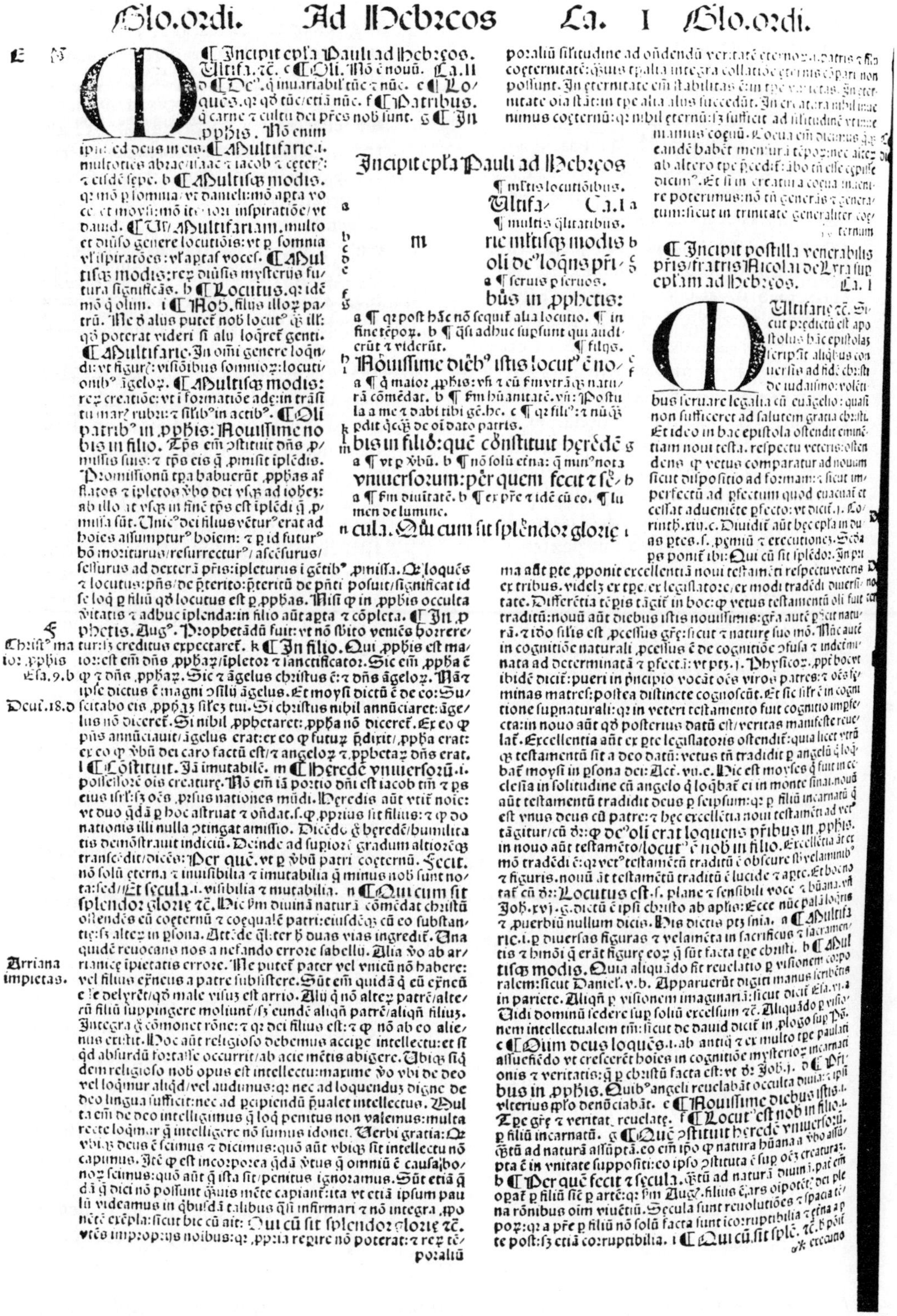
Glo.ordi. Ad Hebreos Ca. I Glo.ordi.

Incipit epl'a Pauli ad Hebreos

VI. Cat. 42. *The corresponding page from a reset volume of the same text, also dated Basel, 3 March 1508 (Photograph by David George)*

INCIPIT SOLLEMNIS repeticio. c. quoniam de electio. libro sexto per eximium ii. doc. sacrorumq; canonu; vez interpretē Do. Staphanū de ayeta de neapoli in qua tractatur iuris patronatus materia.

VONIAM Summa. ut in glo. uel breuius cōfirmacio electionis seu istitucio pñtacionis fiet pmissis uocationibus h.d. Et primo ponit confirmantium abusum quem ꝓhibet cū decreto secūdo ponit uocacionis formam ibi uocationem tercio ad electionem concordem hec ꝓrogat ibi que etiā quod a iu corrigat non dico reꝓbet hēt in glo. dicebam9 fm io. an. in nouella Ali bi dīc ꝙ reꝓbat non corrigit ut nota in c. statutum de pben. in v̄bo declaramus ¶ Nota ꝙ actus cōfirmatōis spectat ad supiorē ut. s̄. co. uenerabilē ¶ itē nota ꝙ ꝓ ocium oclāt mētē statuētꝰ ná istud principiū loquit̄ in elcōe discordi & ita in el ligebat̄ illa ɔltō nisi ī fine fuissꝫ extensa ad electionem cōcordeꝫ cōcordat. l. fi. ff. de here. insti. & qd nota bal. in. l. una ¶. de no. ¶ cōfir ¶ itē nota ꝙ iudex nō debet esse nimis festinus & celer ad ꝓferē dam sentēciam de resti. in int̄ cū ex litteris de sen. & re. iudi. cum eterni. debꝫ g° ꝓcedere cum cāe cognicione l. in cāe s̄. cā cognita ff. de mino. & ¶. comi. uel eptas per totum Et siquidem appareāt iudicii sollemnia ꝓsumit̄ cause cognicio adhibita bar. in. l. ꝓlatam ¶. de sen ¶ Itē nota ꝙ inordinatus affectus & appetitus est cōtrarius equitati & sic cōnectens aliquid equitati arbitreꝝ intendit excludere in ordinatum appetituꝫ fꝫ. d. domi. ¶ Iteꝫ nota ꝙ ille or alium supplantare q facit actum sine uocacione pt s cui p̄iudicat̄ & non discussio negocio fm domi. ꝓ hoc qd nota in. c. cum olim de do. & cōtu. in glo. ii. & iii. & p antibo. d butri. ibi. v. colūp vñ actus dr repentinus quia fit sine citacione & cognicōe requisita xlviii. di. per totam ¶ Item nota ꝙ tex. iste r̄quirit copulatiue uocacionem & discussionem negocii vñ non sufficit alteꝝ adhibere cuꝫ subdat ttes zc̄ licet g° fieret citacio sinō discutit̄ negociū non valꝫ cōfir° ut hic fꝫ o. an. & domi. Lapus dicit hic ꝙ citacione rite facta ut hic tradit̄ absq; alia cē cognicione tꝫ cōfirmacio non ē tenciosa ad hec quod nota io. an. s̄. eo. c. d sicud. v colūp. v̄. sed q̄ritur & de ethico excōmu. si celebret sup v° r̄citanda circa fi. v̄si. si tñ superior fm lapuꝫ & pe. de anch. Aduerte io. an. ibi refert inno. & cōpost. dicentes ꝙ cōfir° sñ cē cognicōe fieri pōt vbi nullus est contradictor uel possessor als cōfirmatus zc̄ & subdit dic ut de electio c. ulti. li. vi. z sic illd ꝓcedebat olī hodie fuari debet hec cōstitucio ut dicet̄ in glo dicebamus & sic supior ex offō tenet̄ examinare p̄sonam electi ē: nem̄ie opponēte ut in. c. cum nobis olim s̄. eo. Et idem dicit ibi do. francis. de ꝫaba de fōrā electionis per illud. c. qsi uelit ꝙ illud. c. req rat etiā cause cognicōꝫ ut dic io. an. Pro hoc quia si requiritur discussio ut s̄. ergo examinacio & cāe cognicio ut in. c. si forte & qs ibi p archi. s̄. eo ti. z li. Et dato ꝙ io. an. in dictis locis assenserit illi dicto tñ dictum suuꝫ hic fuit ultimū q̄a ī prin. huius. c. dicit sic quia decretalis ista multum practicatur cōcepi ultra glo. alioꝝ uel meas ipsius v̄ba discutere Vel dicentum ꝙ io. an. in dictis locis alt. p lapū nō bene dixerit ut dicā sup glo. in v° manes vñ seruatur in practica ꝙ ēt si nullus contradicōr ad edictū cōpareat accusat̄ cōtumacia oīm nō ɔparenciū nec se oponēciū z nōmi9 dat̄ electo seu pñtato termī9 ad ꝓbanduꝫ incūbencia & ipse ꝓbar̄ hꝫ ad finem obtinendi confirmacōꝫ seu ī stitucionem & ꝓbat̄ in. d. c. cum nobis olim & p fre. 9° lvi. Incipit in xpi noīe amen uacante & fran. in. c. i. de postu. p̄la. prima op. ubi uide de forma huius inquisicionis ¶ Itē nota ꝙ dn̄i ap li allari pōt ꝓ iure s. te in. d. c. cū nobis & i. ti. ꝓximo. c i. ¶ item nota ꝙ tales cōfirmaciones q quibus s̄. nullis uocatis & negō non discussio sunt irrite & inanes si g° supior non confirmat sed cassat electionem sine citacione ualebit & bñ facit ipsam cassando si uidet eam non canonicā vñ tex. iste nō habebit locum in īfirmacōe fm io. an. & domi. & . ꝑ e. qui ēt dicūt ꝙ si supior recipit informaciones de his que ēt nemīe opponente debꝫ inquirere ut nota s̄. eo.

VII. Cat. 302. Incipit of Stephanus de Caieta: Repetitio c. quoniam, *Naples, c.1476. The work is recorded as issued by the press, but no other copy has been located (Photograph by David George)*

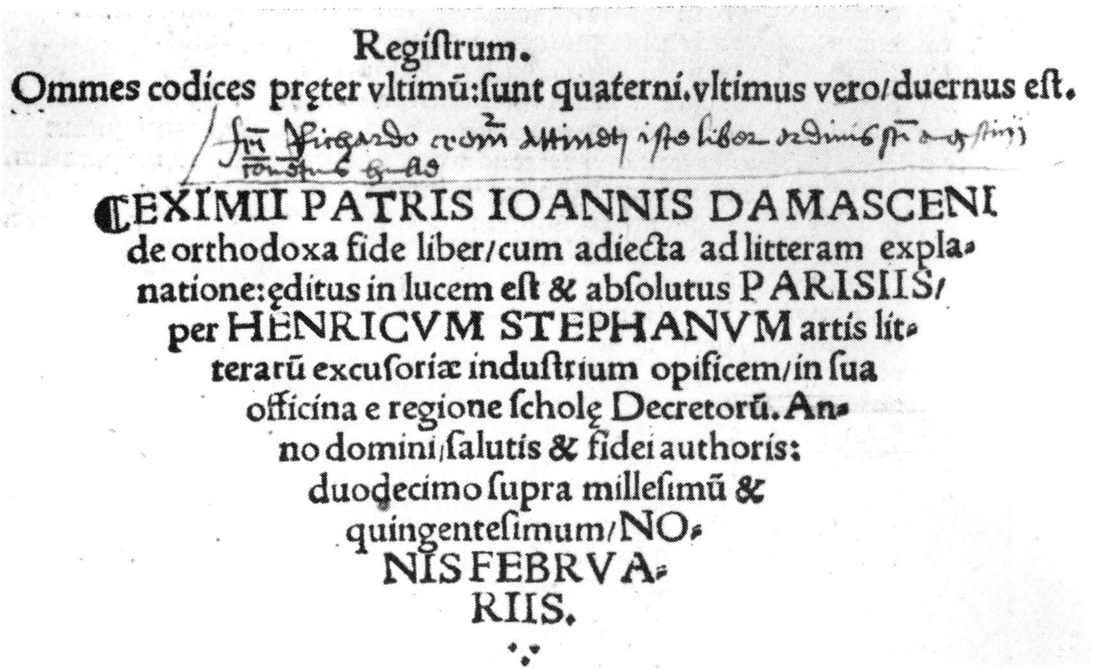

Registrum.
Ommes codices pręter vltimũ:sunt quaterni.vltimus vero/duernus est.

¶EXIMII PATRIS IOANNIS DAMASCENI
de orthodoxa fide liber/cum adiecta ad litteram expla-
natione:ęditus in lucem est & absolutus PARISIIS/
per HENRICVM STEPHANVM artis lit-
terarũ excusoriæ industrium opificem/in sua
officina e regione scholę Decretorũ. An-
no domini/salutis & fidei authoris:
duodecimo supra millesimũ &
quingentesimum/NO-
NIS FEBRVA-
RIIS.

VIIIa. Cat. 190. Colophon of St John of Damascus: De orthodoxa fide, Paris, 1512, with inscription linking the book to the Augustinian Friary at Hull. No other volume of this house is recorded (Photograph by David George)

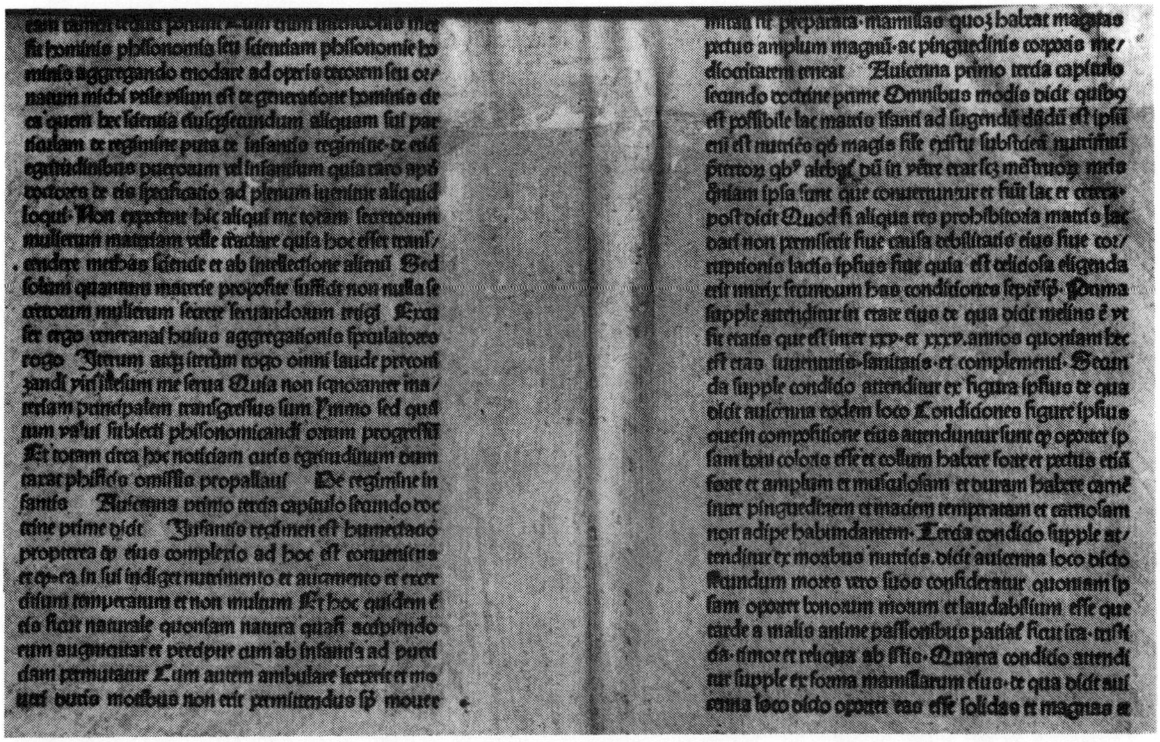

VIIIb. End paper of Cat. 190, two pages (f.lxxv verso and f.lxviii recto) from a section no longer extant of Cornelius Roelans: De aegritudinibus infantium, Louvain, 1486 (Photograph by David George)

Quarta figura.

¶ Hec figura seruit qrto capitulo: In qua circulus principalis repñsentat orbẽ lune [illegible]
fra quẽ sunt quattuor elemẽta ⁊ õnia generabilia ⁊ corruptibilia. ¶ Ignis ẽ [illegible]
siccus immediate post sperã lune situatꝫ: ubi tam purꝰ ⁊ clarꝰ q̄ ẽ inuisibilis. ¶ [illegible]
calidꝰ ⁊ humidus in tres regiones diuisꝰ. Quaꝝ supma spere ignis iungitur ⁊ [illegible]
cũ celo de oriente in occidentẽ mouet̃. ¶ Aqua ẽ frigida ⁊ humida q̃ inter aerem ⁊ terra
naturaliter situatur. Sed tñ vna pars terre q̃ ẽ minus grauis q̄ alia supeminet ⁊ pro
magna portione discooperit̃ aquis vt sit habitabilis. ¶ Maxima ãt pfunditas oceani
ẽ.xiiii.miliariũ vt quidã a marinariis inuentũ eẽ asserũt. Dicẽtes etiã q̄ eadẽ profundi
tas minor ẽ q̄ dupla ad distantiã centri mũdi ⁊ cẽtri terre. ¶ Terra ẽ frigida ⁊ sicca q̄
figurã habet quasi rotundã. Cuius circuitꝰ cõtinet. CCC lx. portiones totidẽ gradibꝰ ce
li correspõdentes: ⁊ cuilibet gradui correspõdent in terra septingẽta stadia: quoꝝ octo
valẽt miliare: ⁊ duo miliaria leucã. Vnde cõcludunt aliqui totũ circuitũ terre continere
quindecim millia septingenta ⁊ quinquaginta leucas.

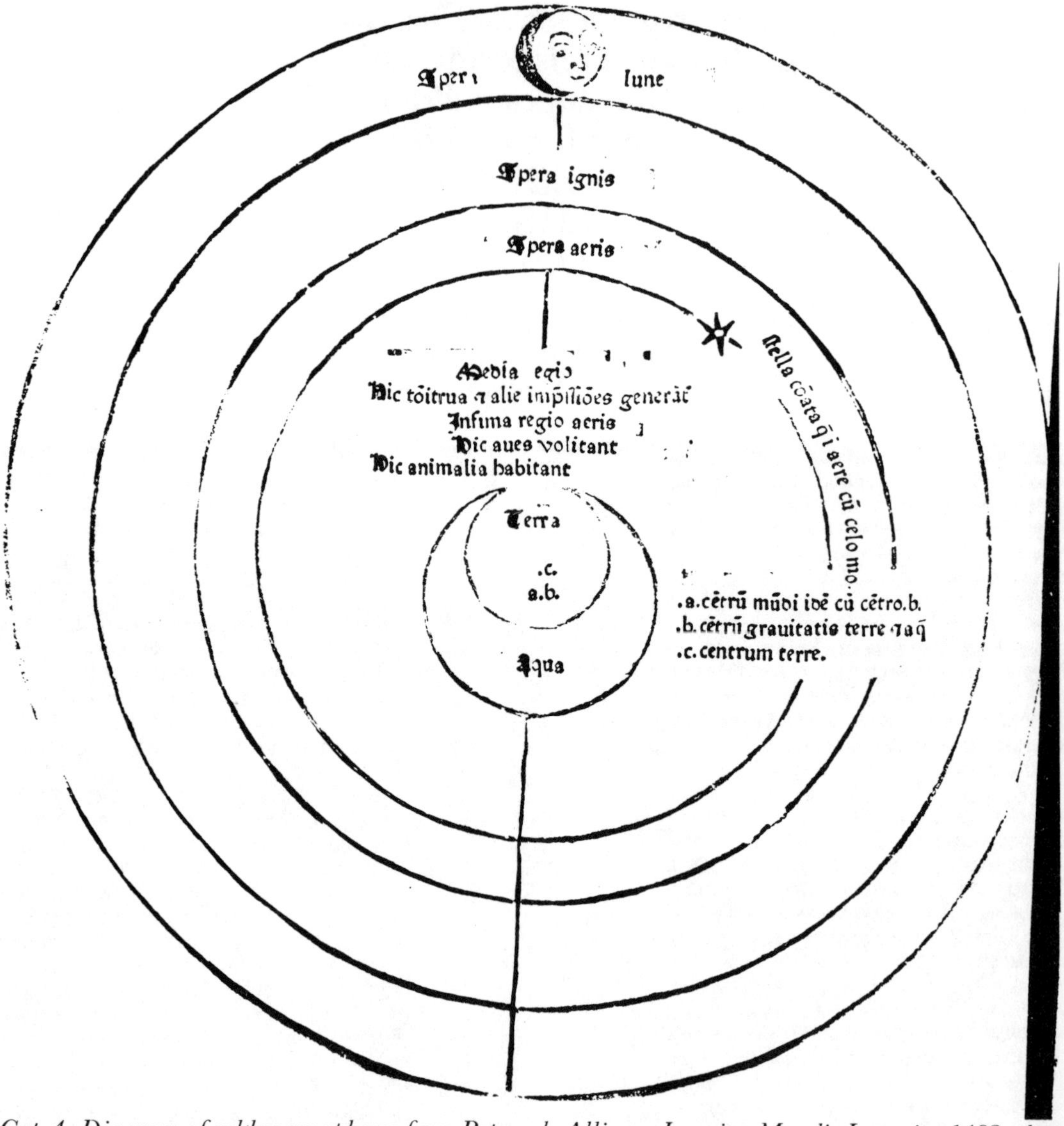

IX. Cat. 4. Diagram of sublunary spheres from Petrus de Alliaco: Imagine Mundi. Louvain, 1483, showing displacement of the aqueous sphere to allow emergence of habitable dry land. A comet circulates in the upper atmosphere. The circumference of the terrestrial sphere is overestimated by about 16 per cent. The legends are overprinted on the woodcut figures.

(Photograph by David George)

Index of Printers and Booksellers

Two or more houses associated with one book are entered separately. Any dates given cover years when the printer was active but are not otherwise definitive. English booksellers are shown by 'for' in brackets.

Provenance Index

Where legible signatures are found in books they are given in the text with other information selected from any inscriptions that accompany them. Information in brackets is taken from external reference sources and not from the books themselves.

Some signatures are graffiti scribbled on blank pages or end papers, but they are of local interest and are included in this index. Donors are also listed.

APPENDIX I

The Catalogus Librorum, 1608

The original manuscript is now in the Lincolnshire Archives Office, Ref. Grantham (St Wulfram) Parish 23/4. The list is on parchment in a clear Italianate hand although the elaborately monogrammed signature has not yet been deciphered. The writer was evidently not an experienced scrivener and failed to rule up his parchment; as a result the writing, in his efforts to get the material on the sheet, becomes progressively smaller and more closely spaced. In the end a shorter fourth column is included although the first occupies one third of the width available. The first transcription, Bodleian MS Eng Misc. C.360, was made in 1957 by Dorothy Owen, then of the Archives Office.

It has now (November 1986) been reworked completely by Joan Williams and Nicholas Bennet, who have tried to reproduce exactly the details of the original apart from the progressive compression. The use of the punctuation marks . , : and / is as in the text; so is the spacing and the run-on of lines. The headings printed in bold are in a larger and more elaborate script, possibly written with a different quill. Standard abbreviations are expanded in square brackets, although that for final -us is transcribed without comment. The initial written with a loop is rendered as J, with a small cross stroke as I. The (presumably decorative) marks resembling ampersands are represented as such. The order in the list, with most of the volumes in the Trigge bequest (marked †) grouped together, probably records the arrangement on the original benches in 1608. Joan Williams suggests that the marginal numbers [1], 2, 3, 4, now included in the transcription for the first time, may refer to these benches.

The present catalogue numbers of extant books are added for reference.

Catalogus Librorum in Bibliotheca Granthamie, ex dono venerabilis viri Francisci Trigge Rectoris Ecclesie de Welborne/

[Column 1]	Catalogue 1987
Beza/	
In nouum Testamentum	
graeco latine	44
De passione Chr[ist]i	37
Eius opuscula/	38
Caluinus	
In quinque Libros Moses &	
in Joshu:	68
Conciones in Deutrino.	73
Conciones in Job:	74
In psalmos,	65
In Esaiam	63
In Jeremian	72
In Exechiel' & Daniel'	70, 71
In prophetas minores	69
In om[n]es Epistolas.	67
Harmonia in Evangelistas.	66
Tractatus theologoci om[n]es	75
Marolatus	
In Genesim/	not extant

In Evangelia & Act'.	227.1
In Epist: pauli & Canonicas/	227.2
Zancheus	
De natura dei	349
De Tribus Elohim.	351
De operibus dei.	350
De Redemptione	355
De Incarnatione.	348
De doctrina Christiana	347
In epist: ad Ephes': philip'.	352
Col: Thessal'.	353
Missellanea.	354
Fides/	not extant
Wolfangus [sic]	
Musculus	
In Genesim.	259
In psalmos.	260
In Esaiam.	257
In Mathaeum.	258
In Ioannem.	253
In Epist: ad Rom: Galat:	252, 254
Ephes': Phil: Coll': Thes: & Timoth:	255, 256
Loci com[m]unhes.	261
Junius	
De Trinitate:	194
In Genesim & Exod:	197, 198
In Ionam & Daniel':	195, 196
Joannes King in Ionam.	201
Crastouij Bellu[m] Jesuiticu[m]	84
Lubbertus	
De papa Romana.	223
De principijs Chr[ist]ianorum dogmatum./	224
Andradij Orthodox:	8
Whittakerus & Rainoldus	334, 335, 276
Conciones Funebres &	55
Nuptiales./	56
Bonauentura in Lucam.	54
Stella in Lucam.	300
Serranus in Leuit & Ezech:	288, 289
Masius in Ioshu:	228
Ephiphanius contra hereses.	not extant
Leonis pape opera	214
Rabbanus in Genesim & Exod:	180
Dandrada contra Chemnitium.	7
Arnobius in om[n]es psalmos & Adversus gentes	22
Licosthenis similia.	225
Marlaeus in Hest:	not extant
Danaeus	
In Symbolum Apostoloru[m].	not extant
In prophetas minores.	93
Antiquitatu[m] Sectiones lib: 4.	96
Isagog: Chr[ist]iana, volu: 2	92
Polit' Christ'	95

[Column 2]

Danaeus	
De sacramentis contra Bellarmi:	90
De membris eccl[es]ie militant' contra	91
Bellarminu[m] 2. lib:	
Opuscula.	94
Chemnitius	
Harmonia – 2	81
Loci Theologici: vol 2	82 (3 vols)
Examen Concilij Tridentini	80
Loci com[m]unes./	
Baliei Centurie	28
Caroli Sigonij historiae.	293
Rem: Testamentum/	not extant
Ferus	
In Exod: Num. Deut. Joshu. Judices.	140
In Job:	145
In Matheum.	143
In Joannem.	144
In Acta:	141
Epitome sermonum &	142
Adraee Musculi loci com[m]unes	251
Ursinus in Esaiam.	not extant
Ribera in omnes prophetas	281
Wolsius [sic]	
In: Deut: Ioshu: & Ezram	342, 343, 345
In Iudices & Ruth.	344
In Nehemiam.	346
De Tempore.	341
Pintus	
In Esaiam.	not extant
In Ezechielem.	270
In Lamenta: Daniel' & Nahum./	269
Gualterus	
In Esaiam.	166
In p[ro]phetas minores.	167
In Lucam	165
In Acta:	162
In Rom: & Galat:	163, 164
Lauaterus	
In Ioshu: Iudic: & Iob.	205, 208, 209
In P[ro]uerb Ecclesiast: & Ezech:	206, 212

In paralipomenon 204
In Ezram: cont. a/. cu[m] Erast: 212
de excom[m]unica[ti]o[n]e 137
2. Thesaurus lingue s[an]c[t]e Autore Pagnino./ not extant
Gerardi Herbal'. not extant
Textoris officina. 278
Cornelij Celci Medicina. 77
Weckeri Antidoton. 331
Weckeri Sintaxis. 332

Gesnerus

De Quadrupedibus. 152.1
De volatilibus.
De Aquatilibus. 152.2

Berchorius.

Reuertorium. 33
Reductorium. 34
Rhoderigij Lectiones Antique 280

Albertus.

Postilla in Marcum & Ioan[n]em. 1, 3
Postilla in Lucam. 2

Arius Montanus.

Biblia sacra hebraice Chaldaice graece & latine 39 (4 vols, three extant)
In duodecim p[ro]phetas 21
Testamentu[m] nouum Syriace graece & latine editum a Guidone Fabritio. not extant
Apparatus Bibliorum (3 vols, none extant)
Biblia Int[r]. linear. 40
Concordantia hebraice not extant
Concordantia graece 302
Concordantia latine 301

[Column 3]

Foxus.

Martyrum Liber 150
In Apocalypsim meditationes 149
&
Chronicon Hollingshed volum: 2. not extant
Historiaru[m] Ecclesiast: Centur. 13. volum. 8. 226
Concilioru[m] Tomi. 4. vol: 4.
Polidorus Virgilius hist: Angl: 320
Rosinus de Antiquitate Rom: 280
Nouuus [sic] orbis. 161
Thesaurus Conciniatorum
Hospinianus de origine Monichatus 179

Bucerus

In Psalmos: Judic: & Sophonia[m]. 58, 60
In Rom: & Ephes: 57, 59
&
Sadielis opera. 285
Speculum vincentij vol: 4 329
Petrus Lombardus 266
Alfonsus aduersus om[n]es hereses not extant

Thomas Aquinas

In Evangelia. 15
In Epist: Pauli 16
Postilla in Genesim. 17
&
Iansenii harmonia in Evangelist: 188
Bellarmini Controversiae, Tomis tribus volum. 4 32
Senecae opera. 287
Flauij Iosephi opera 192
Iustini Martyris opera graece & latine 200
Diui Clementis Recognitio[n]es not extant
Clementis Alexandrini op[er]a. 87
Clemens, Ireneus & philo Judeus.vno vol. 86

Origines

In vetus testamentum.
In Nouum testamentum. 264
&
Tertulliani opera. 311
Cyprianus. 88
Athanasij opera. 23
Gregorij Nazianzeni opera. 160
.38.
Eusebij pamphilij opera. 139
Basilij magni opera. 30
Christostomi Tomi quinque & vol: 3[a]. 83
Theodoreti opera. 313
Hieronomi Tom. 9 & vol: 3[a]. 189
Ambrosij Tomi quinque & vol: 2. 6
Augustini Tomi decem. & vol: 5 24
Gregorij magni opera 158
Nycephori histor: ecclesiast: 262
Hillarij opera/ 176
Barnardi opera. 36
Cyrilli opera. 89
Damasceni opera. 190
Lyranus in Vetus & nouu[m] testamentum vo. 7. 41
Dionisias in Evangelia. 99
† Annales eccl[es]isie [sic] autore Baronio volum: 6 29

Blasius in Apocalypsim Joannis 327
Phillippi Diez: opera volum: 7 97, 98 (6 vols extant)
Theatrum humanae vitae vol: 9 lib. 4 356
Autore Theodor Zuingero.

† **S**coti opera. lib. 2. 101 with 102, 103 with 104

Antoninus.

Eius sum[m]a 14
Tres eius Libri historial':, lib: 1: 13
Catholicon, Autore f[rat]re Joanne 27
Synopsis papismi, Autore Willetto. 338
Tetrastilon papismi not extant
Lyra in om[n]es epist: 42 (?)
&
:. Thesaurus graece lingue Lib: 3.
Autore Stephano. not extant

Hemingius

In pslalmos [sic] not extant
In Joannem. 172
In Epist: 171
Opuscula. 173

Marcerus

In Genesim. 239
In Iob: P[ro]uerb: Eccl[es]en & Cant: 236, 237
In p[ro]phetas minores. 238

Petrus Martyr:

In Genesim. 324
In Judices. 325
In Lib: Samuelis 322
In lib: Regum. 326
In Romanos. 323
In: I. Corinth. 321

[Column 4]

Mollerus

In Esaiam 242
In psalmos: 291

Bullingerus

In Daniel'. 61
In Jeremiam vna
cu[m] Altercatione. 62
Synagogue cu[m] eccl[es]ia. 5
Oleaster in Pentateuchon. 175
Oeconomia Biblioru[m] Autore Edero. 107
Problemata Theolog: Aretij. 19
Institutiones viguerij 328
Loci co[mmun]es Szegedini. 309
&
Decretalia Gregoij 159
Decretalia Gratiani. 157
Wesembecius in pandect: Iuris ciuilis 333
Decreta Nicolai panormit'. 317
Repeticio Lanfranci de Oriano. 202
Sermones quadrage simales de legibus Autore f[rat]re Leonardo 215
Rep[er]toriu[m] Ioannis Milis. 240
Plowdons reports. 271, 272
Fitzherberts. 147
La grand Abridgm[en]t.
Tabulae 148

De Terminis regnante. Ed[wa]r[d]o: 3°. lib:.2°. 108–116, 117
De Terminis Regnantibus Edw: 5.to Ric[ard]o. 3°. & Hen: 7°./ 133–136
De terminis regnante Hen: 6to 118–131
Imago mundi, Autore Ioanne Gersone. 4
Jacobi Latomi Theologia 203
Summa Angelica 10
Bartholomeus Anglicus de p[ro]prietatibus rerum. not extant
Rationale diuinoru[m] 105
The answer to ye. Admonicion'. 336

Exscript' p[er]me.
Jo: [?]: Feb: 1608

APPENDIX 2

A note on signatures and collations for subscribers to this catalogue.

Books are not printed a page at a time. A number of blocks of type are impressed on a sheet, which is afterwards folded to form pages and then (traditionally) sewn to a backing along with its fellows to make up a volume. The simplest arrangement is the folio, which has two blocks of print on each side of a sheet folded in two to give a section of two leaves or four pages of the final book.

The printing press, however, was organised by mass production right from the start. Perhaps 500 sheets would have been printed with two pages of type before re-setting the press with the blocks (or *formes*) of type for the two pages on the reverse side, and at the end of the run the folder would have many stacks of sheets to put together in order. An early innovation was to print, on the bottom of what would be the first page in a folded section, a letter of the alphabet, A–Z omitting J, V, W. These letters were called signatures.

If there were more than 23 sheets there would be a second set of signatures Aa–Zz, and so on. The folder would then pick up the sheets alphabetically. The binder in turn deals with the folded sections, again checking the order easily by the signatures. Since each folded section has two leaves we would write down the *collation* of a book as, say

$A–Z^2 \quad Aa–Zz^2 \quad Aaa–Hhh^2$

this book would have 23 + 23 + 8 sections, 108 leaves, 216 pages.

Each section had to be sewn separately, and it soon became convenient to arrange the pages so that 2, 3 or more sheets could be folded together to make sections of 8, 12 or more pages. This needed careful planning and setting of the formes of type and was called 'imposition' by the printers. The first section of a book sewn in threes would have, on one side of its first sheet pp. 1, 12 and on the other 2, 11. The folder would need to keep track of the sheets within each section, so they were numbered as well as lettered to give A1, A2, A3 . . . The printer, for a three sheet section, would often put A4 on the reverse of A3, so that the folder would know when to stop gathering sheets and begin folding. If you examine some of our books you will see, on the right hand pages the signatures A1 . . . A4 followed by two without signatures, then B1 . . . B4 followed by blanks and so on. There are now six leaves to a section, and a book could be collated as

$A–Z^6 \quad Aa–Pp^6$

with 38 sections and 456 pages.

Titles, dedications, indexes and so on were usually printed after the text and signed separately, so that the complete collation of a book could be, say

$☆^4 \quad ☆☆^4 \quad A–M^6 \quad N^4 \quad O–Z^6 \quad Aa–Pp^6 \quad a^8$

The change between M and O means that for some reason, such as a decision to change presses or compositors, signature N was planned with only two sheets or four leaves. Analysis of collations gives many clues to the work of the early master printers, and this is why we take them off. The folio is the simplest fold, and results in the largest book. If four pages are set on each side of a sheet afterwards folded twice into eight page sections the result is a quarto, if eight pages per side with four folds, an octavo, and so on. These are written 4°, 8° and collated, as before, by the number of leaves in a section. Thus a quarto book could be

$A\text{–}Z^4 \quad Aa\text{–}Qq^4$

Since the four leaves are made by folding only one sheet, a quarto book will show the signatures A, B, C . . . on pages followed by three without signatures; an octavo has seven blanks, and so on. The tops of pairs of pages of a quarto are joined, and need to be cut by the reader or trimmed by the binder.

There are various complications in the analysis of many books, but this note should help those who would otherwise find the collation lines unintelligible, as indeed they were to us when we began our catalogue.

A note on imprints

The names of printers and towns are often found in latinized forms. Some English equivalents in place-names are obvious, as Antuerpia = Antwerp, Morgiis = Morges; but some others are likely to be unfamiliar. A short list follows:

Argentina	Strassburg
Basilea	Basle
Colonia Agrippina	Cologne
Erfordia	Erfurt
Lovanium	Louvain
Lugdunum	Lyons
Lugdunum Batavorum	Leyden
Lutetia	Paris
Mediolanum	Milan
Moguntia	Mainz
Panormum	Palermo
Rothomagum	Rouen
Tiguri	Zürich
Venetiae	Venice

The terms *ex officina*, *in aedibus* and *apud* before the names of printers are equivalent to 'at the workshop or establishment of' – the French 'chez'. The words *sumptibus*, and *impensis* mean 'at the expense of', the equivalent of 'for' in an English imprint.

APPENDIX 3

Sixteenth century price codes

In an article on the Ipswich Town Library published in *The Book Collector*, vol. 35 no. 2, Summer 1986, pp. 191–8, J. M. Blatchly calls attention to handwritten letters or small groups of letters on the title pages of books, usually beside or just below the imprint. The Library possesses a Benefactors' Book which records the prices paid for some of the earlier volumes, and by examining these Dr Blatchly has concluded that the letters are booksellers' price codes, commonly the very simple code a = 1, b = 2, . . .

His library has twenty-six titles with such letter groups: the Trigge Library seems to have about sixty, mostly dated towards the end of the sixteenth century. As in Ipswich multi-volume works have the code on the first volume only. Some of the letters are not easy to decipher, but Dr Blatchly has supplied his conjectured equivalents for nearly forty of them. Others have been added.

Catalogue number	Author	Date	Mark	Blatchly code £	s.	d.
7	Andrada	1580	c		3	0
15	Aquinas	1566	fb		6	2
17		1573	a	1	0	0
22	Arnobius	1560	af	1	6	0
23	Athanasius	1581	Lh		11	8
29*	Baronius (6 vols)	1601–7	e	5	0	0
32	Bellarmine (vol. 2)	1597	nd		13	4
36	Bernardus	1586	fB		6	2
37	Beza	1592	mB		12	2
45		1585	fB		6	2
56	Brandmiller	1603	B		2	0
63	Calvin	1583	f		6	0
67		1580	hd		8	4
68		1595	n:.			
70		1583	d		4	0
72		1589	hd		8	4
75		1597	P		15	0
80	Chemnitius	1585	jf		9	6
81		1593	fh		6	8
82	(3 vols)	1594	R		17	0
84	Chrastorius	1593	C		3	0
91	Danaeus	1598	bf		2	6
92		1588	fh e			
93		1586	ch		3	8

94		1583	3–5	
96		1596	af	1 6
98	Diez	1600	k	10 0
138	Eusebius	1619	g	7 0
142	Ferus	1561	m 12 (decoded?)	12 0
153*	Glass (3 vols)	1651	14ff	
162	Gualtherus	1555	fh	6 8
172	Hemmingius	1590	e	5 0
173		1586	fh	6 8
176	Hilary	1570	e	5 0
188	Jansen	1591	9	
214	Leo Magnus	1583	C	3 0
244	Lubbertus	1591	1 E (?)	
226*	Magdeburg Centuriators (8 vols)	1560–74	bk	2 10 0
238	Mercerus	1570	fh	6 8
239	Mercerus	1598	nd	13 4
241	Moller	1591	P	15 0
242		1588	e	5 0
256	Musculus	1569	k	10 0
258		1578	e	5 0
267	Peter Lombard	1566	bpge (?)	
285	Sadeel	1593	7–6	7 6
301	Stephanus	1594	k	10 0
319	Ursinus	1589	fc	6 3
321	Vermigli	1579	d	4 0
323		1588	s (?)	
326		1581	f–gf	
331	Wecker	1588	e	5 0
344	Wolfius	1598	cd	3 4
346		1570	b	2 0
347	Zanchius	1598	a 7	
349		1598	fd	6 4
353		1594	k	10 0
354		1592	e	5 0

Multi-volume works marked on the first volume only are starred. The interpretations could only be verified if we had accounts of prices actually paid, but most of them are reasonable and consistent. Clearly 13s. 4d. is one mark, and fh = 6s. 8d. is half a mark. The value ch = 3s. 8d. suggests a misreading of cd = 3s. 4d. Blanks have been left where the simple Blatchly code seems inapplicable, and it is to be hoped that further information will eventually be available.